30-DAY
KICKASS
SINGLE MOM
Money Makeover

30-Day Kickass Single Mom Money Makeover
First Edition, October 2018

Like a Mother Media
New York, New York

Editing: Shayla Raquel, ShaylaRaquel.com
Publishing and Design Services: Melinda Martin, MelindaMartin.me

ISBN: 978-1-7328009-2-2 (paperback), 978-1-7328009-1-5 (epub)

PRAISE FOR

The Kickass Single Mom

*Be Financially Independent, Discover Your Sexiest Self,
and Raise Fabulous, Happy Children*

"A must-read!"

—*New York Post*

"This book will help so many women."

—**Jenny McCarthy**

"It's high time that mothers, just like all women, are embraced and supported to access the power of their sensual truth. In her new book, *The Kickass Single Mom*, Emma Johnson takes a fierce stand for removing the shame and stigma around motherhood, sex, pleasure, and power."

—Regena Thomashauer,
New York Times **Bestselling Author of** *Pussy: A Reclamation*,
Founder of the School of Womanly Arts

"The *Kickass Single Mom* is a much-needed roadmap for the 10 million US single moms to achieving their goals and creating an abundant and happy future for themselves and their kids. Emma Johnson's writing is smart, researched, and hilarious at the same time."

—Jean Chatzky, NBC Today, HerMoney Podcast

"This book is like having a stand-up comic, high-priced divorce attorney, no-nonsense mentor, and perfect best friend by your side as you make the same trek Emma Johnson did: from alone and scared to happy, wealthy, and sexy. Emma's work is a new movement that rebrands single moms for what they really are: competent, capable, sensual, solvent, loving, lovable, and, of course, kickass!"

—Lenore Skenazy,
Founder of the Book and Blog *Free-Range Kids*

"All the single mommies! Get your hands up and get a copy. This book is raw, real, and mandatory reading for the 10 million-plus single moms and the friends and family who love them. Single mom superhero Emma Johnson is redefining what it means to fly solo with kids. She has heard it all, makes no excuses, and pulls no punches in fighting to empower her tribe of single moms."

—Bobbi Rebell, Author of *How to be a Financial Grownup:*
Proven Advice from High Achievers on
How to Live Your Dreams and Have Financial Freedom

30-DAY
KICKASS
SINGLE MOM
Money
Makeover

Get Your Financial Act Together,
FINALLY AND FOREVER!

EMMA JOHNSON

Author of #1 Bestseller *The Kickass Single Mom*
Creator of Wealthysinglemommy.com

As a special thank you for investing in this book (and yourself!), I've included three free chapters of my yet-to-be published book: *WTF Wednesdays: Single Mom Q&A on Money, Sex, Parenting and Life*. Skip to page 151 to get a sneak-peek of the book based on my popular blog column: WTF Wednesdays. Enjoy!

For my moms

TABLE OF CONTENTS

Introduction

Hey, Mama!

I have been interacting daily with single moms around the world for six years, ever since launching Wealthysinglemommy.com. The site started as a personal blog, where I worked out my experiences and challenges as an unmarried mom who was dating, building a business, dealing with an ex, and figuring out her new life. I also heavily reflected on my own experience growing up with a divorced, single mom—at the height of the 1980s divorce boom, as well as the first wave of women entering the professional workforce en masse.

My initial months and years facing single motherhood were riddled with very familiar fears, rooting back to my childhood—I was terrified of living out of my car with two tiny children. Even if homelessness didn't go down, I was horrified of living just as my mother did: always broke, that tension of poverty hanging forever over the house like a blanket of nervous electricity, my children disappointed that as an educated, white, middle-class woman, *I couldn't get my act together already.*

Thankfully, I was able to get on my feet, to shake off child support within a year of my breakup, and to run a thriving online business, of which the sole goal is to help women recognize their power and build incredible lives for themselves and their families—no matter what that family looks like.

The No. 1 part of making this goal a reality is money. I constantly ask women who follow me what their biggest challenge is, and 99 percent of the time, the answer is: *I don't have enough money.*

The roots of this issue are deep, cultural, societal, and political. They are also internal, inside each woman. And I know that they can be changed in each woman reading this. I know this not only because I have experienced it personally, but also because I have connected with literally hundreds of thousands of single moms, or women considering becoming a single mom, who have overcome habits, mindsets, and practices that have held them back financially and professionally. So many have reached out and shared that with surprisingly small changes, their money, and as a result their *lives*, changed dramatically, often within a stunningly short period.

Now, I am not in the business of promising magic, or even overnight results. Building a successful business and career, as well as wealth, requires time and dedication. But the biggest obstacles to these challenges are bad daily habits and your mindset—things that *can* turn around overnight.

That's what this book is about. In as short as one month, you will tackle every single major part of financial wellness—most of all, the way you think about and act around money. It's not all mindset and intention. The *30-Day Kickass Single Mom Money Makeover* is also about the real, practical steps to getting your financial act together. This month will get you on track to control your spending, start saving and investing, and turn around your debt and credit score.

In short, if you follow these steps every day, each of which typically takes fewer than ten minutes, you will thrust your spending, earning, and saving on a powerful, positive trajectory—*which will change your life forever.*

Are you ready? Of course you are—you bought the damn book!

Let's do this!

XO,

Emma

P.S. Don't forget to get your free gift, three free chapters of my yet-to-be published book: *WTF Wednesdays: Single Mom Q&A on Money, Sex, Parenting and Life*. Skip to page 151 to get a sneak-peek of the book based on my popular blog column: WTF Wednesdays!

P.P.S. Since you're reading this in paperback, I've included a resources page on my website for every single link that's used here. You can find every link here: Wealthysinglemommy. com/resources.

DAY 1

Kickass Single Mom
Money Makeover!

Hey, Mama!

I am so grateful you joined the *30-Day Kickass Single Mom Money Makeover*. Here you will find 30 daily challenges requiring you to take action to improve one element of your finances. We will tackle debt, that emergency fund, new ways to save money each month, your career and income, investing and saving for the future, and more. Lots more. Your mind will melt by the amount of movement you can achieve in your bank account in one month *when you really focus and take action.*

I will be with you every step of the way. Cheesy but true:

today is the first day of the rest of your life. Which brings me to today's action step . . .

Today, I want you to *own* your money situation. This means to take stock of how you feel about money, understand why you do not earn, save, and invest like you know you should, and the number-one biggest source of stress when it comes to money. The very frustrating fact is that most women do not feel good about money. We are taught from a very young age that money is impolite, taboo, that it's best to leave the earning and managing of money to men (otherwise, they are emasculated and will leave us, we are told. To which I say: *whatever.*), that if we seek, ask for, and enjoy money, we are greedy gold-diggers and materialistic.

EFF ALL OF THAT.

This is the truth: money is power. Without enough money, you spend your energy and time on stressing about money. When you do not have control of your money, you do not control your life. That compromises every part of your existence: parenting, career decisions, health, relationships—and how you manage your money!

I want you to feel confident when you think about money. I want you to sense joy when you manage your money. I want you to have an overall sense of abundance in every part of your life. That is impossible when you feel broke and stuck.

Today is the hardest day of the challenge because your assignment has three parts (the rest of the days have just one task plus one battlecry—a phrase I want you to shout out loud, to think about, and stew on). Here we go!

TODAY'S BATTLECRY

"I LOVE MONEY!"

Say it at least three times, as loud as you can muster. Public or private, no matter. Own it. Own that money is powerful and you deserve to feel amazing about money. Maybe today you don't love money. Maybe money makes you squirm or want to turn away and wish it didn't exist. Maybe you try to tell yourself that money is the construct of the patriarchy, designed to control and manipulate the vulnerable. Maybe that is true, I don't know. But I do know this: you can't torpedo the patriarchy or serve the vulnerable if you are broke and worried about paying the rent. So I will help you get over all that and learn to adore money and the power that comes with it.

TODAY'S TASKS

Note: You don't need an expensive leather-bound notebook. Any scrap of paper will do. Save a polar bear and reuse the back of all that crap they send home in your kid's school folder, or the margins of the newspaper. The point is to physically write it down. Powerful!

1. Write down your first, or most powerful, money memory. Ideas about who we are and how we manage our finances (and every other part of our lives, for that matter) are rooted in early teachings and experiences. Think about fights your parents had about finances, or messages from teachers, aunts, or grandparents about what women are capable of when it comes to career and money. What stands out the most? Write down the first three that come to mind. This is an incredible first step in taking responsibility for your money situation, as you start to see *why* you think about

money as you do, and how that thinking affects how you *act* around money.

2. Think about your own personal finances. Write down the number-one aspect of your money that gives you the most grief and stress and sucks away time. Debt? Stuck in your career? Not saved yet for retirement? No cash cushion? Write it down and look at it hard. That is your truth. Neither good nor bad. Huge step. Good work!

3. Name your support system. A colleague, your romantic partner, another single mom in your community, or an old friend who lives far away—someone who will hold you accountable to the goals you set and work on during this challenge and beyond. In addition, please post your goals, challenges, and ideas to share in Millionaire Single Moms (Facebook.com/groups/millionairesinglemoms), our wonderful, positive closed Facebook community that's changing single moms' lives.

OK, lady. You did it. Big, hard first day. Hang tight, and I will see you tomorrow.

---------------------------- ☆ ----------------------------

DAY 2

What Is Your Single Mom Money Mindset?

Hey, Mama!

Some of the most impactful studies I have read in recent years is the power of your surroundings. It's a fact that if a teenager spends time with kids who smoke, they are more likely to smoke. If your friends are in debt or overweight, you are likely to be the same. If you have a close friend who's divorced, you are more likely to divorce (something I can attest to myself—for a few years, I referred to myself as the "divorce vector"). In other words, what you see day in and day out becomes your normal—and what you expect of yourself. That's why parenting is so hard: you know that you are a role model for your kids, and the pressure day in and day out is *real*.

If you're a single mom and know you don't live up to your full financial potential, there's a reason for that. Somewhere in your early years—and likely more recent years too!—you absorbed messages about what it meant to be a single mom. There's a very, very excellent chance that that message was negative and always included being broke. Here are some common stereotypes about single moms that you likely received from family members (maybe even your own single mom growing up), the media, people in your community, and even your dearest friends:

★ Single moms should hurry up and find a man who can help pay the bills/take care of the kids/take care of them. (Reality: we are not princesses in towers waiting to be rescued!)

★ Single moms made bad decisions/couldn't keep a man, and get what they deserve. (Reality: shit happens, and life is long and full of ups and downs. Just because your family doesn't look like the Cleavers' family doesn't mean yours is wrong. Plus: forgiveness.)

★ Single moms have to work five jobs just to keep food on the table and the lights on. Life as a single mom is miserable! (Reality: you can work five jobs, or work one really great, high-paying job. Also, life is only miserable if you decide it is.)

★ Single moms are destined to be broke, to become a social pariah with messed-up kids. (I go on and on and on about the research on this in my first book, *The Kickass Single Mom* [Wealthysinglemommy. com/resources], but the reality is that kids of single moms are not statistically worse off than those inside of traditional Cleaver marriages, the majority of new single moms are college educated, and we sure as shizzle are not all broke.)

I appreciate that right now you may indeed be broke. But together over the next few weeks, we'll shake you free of feeling and acting broke and set you on a positive path toward less debt and more income, savings, and wealth.

TODAY'S BATTLECRY

"My family is complete just as it is!
I decide what my single mom identity is!"

TODAY'S TASKS

Write down your earliest memories about a single mom. This might be an unmarried mom in your own family, neighborhood, someone from TV or the movies. I think about my own mom, a few parents in my hometown, Angela from *Who's the Boss?* and the mom from *Good Times*.

Next, write down your impression of this woman. Was it positive or negative? Was she empowered or dependent? A good mom or a harried, stressed-out one? Did she own her sexuality, or was she desperately trying to snag a man—or celibate?

Then, think about how these early messages informed your own ideas about what your life means now that you're a single mom. Focus on the financial parts, but think about your parenting, relationships, and other parts of your life. They are all related.

Write down what you discovered about yourself. Then, share what you learned in Millionaire Single Moms (Facebook.com/groups/millionairesinglemoms) on Facebook!

Tomorrow, we start the down-and-dirty work of getting real with your cash. It will be fun and hard. That's how you know change is happening. See you then!

———————— ☆ ————————

DAY 3

Time to Get Real

Hey, Mama!

Today is the day you have likely been avoiding looking at the cold, hard numbers. Right up in your grill. One of the biggest mistakes I see moms make is that when something is uncomfortable, you avoid it. This is so true about money. Is this you?

Don't open bills.

Ignore your credit score.

Have no idea how much your total debt is.

No idea how much you actually need to save and invest each month to meet your goals.

Ignore interest rates on credit cards, car notes, and other debt.

Clueless about bill due dates.

You're an adult, and it's time to get real with yourself about your true money picture. The truth may hurt like hell, but it's impossible to change your money picture for the better without full-frontal honesty—*with yourself.*

TODAY'S BATTLECRY

"I am ready to be 100 percent honest with myself about my finances! No more fibs or avoiding facts."

Remember to say this out loud!

TODAY'S TASK

Embrace technology.

1. Use an app to connect all your money accounts into one place—checking and savings, investment, credit card, student and car loans, mortgage. Personal Capital (Wealthysinglemommy.com/resources) is a great place to start, and one of my most favorite apps of all time (not just money apps—*all* apps). It gives you a really nice snapshot of your cash and debt in one place. It can be used both on your computer and phone and is 100 percent free and very easy to set up. Tiller (Wealthysinglemommy. com/resources) is also a great app, based on spreadsheets, and comes with a modest monthly fee.

2. Use a goal calculator to be very real with yourself about how far you are from your saving and investing goals. Here is my review of Ellevest

(Wealthysinglemommy.com/resources), which has a totally free financial planner that's specifically designed for women and allows you to assess how far you are from your goals, including retirement, buying a home, starting a business, having a kid, or going for a big splurge—like a trip or home remodel. It takes fewer than four minutes, and is very easy to use.

As you go through this process, a lot is happening. You are looking at the hard numbers. If you *really* do the assignment, and plug all your numbers into your accounts, you see the facts. Once, I was coaching a single mom on working through her financial blocks for a TV segment, and I asked her to give me a rundown of her financial story. She started in on her divorce and the essential oil business she was starting, and then she mentioned a recent bankruptcy—which neither the producers nor I had heard anything about. She quickly turned to the camera woman and threatened, "If you keep my bankruptcy in this story, I will fucking kill you!"

Clearly, she was not ready to be 100 percent honest with anyone, much less herself.

As you are staring at the debts and assets, you will see some patterns and some truths. Write these truths down. The good, the bad, the nasty-ass.

One mom completed this step and emailed me: "I was really surprised to see that I have a six-figure net worth. I feel so broke all the time, and this helped me realize I'm doing better than I thought."

You may also be disgusted by how much debt you have, or how much more you owe on your old car. Avoid judgment on these feelings and facts. Embrace the pain as a necessary step in positive change.

———————————— ☆ ————————————

DAY 4

All the Money

Hey, Mama!

Hooking up all your accounts into Personal Capital or Ellevest (Wealthysinglemommy.com/resources) is so powerful because you just can't argue with those numbers. They're in your face and they don't lie. If you haven't created accounts there, do it now!

However, there's one more thing you need to do to really get *honest* with yourself about your relationship with money—and where your moola is going each day, month, and year.

TODAY'S BATTLECRY

"I am devoted to raising my consciousness about money. I am grateful for the small and large things that money affords my family and me."

TODAY'S TASK

Drill down into those charges on your money app. Really take stock of how much you spend each day, week, and month on things like restaurants, cafes, clothes, unmemorable activities for your kids—like movies at the theater or frivolous trips to the toy store. Then, over the next week, keep track of all the cash you spend. I know that a lot of financial experts recommend paying all cash for everything if you're trying to change your money habits; but I recommend credit or debit cards for all expenses, because it's 100 percent tracked on my Personal Capital (Wealthysinglemommy.com/resources), so I see it all in one place.

For things you pay in cash, like coffee, field trip fees for your kids, parking meters—everything else— write them down and plug them into your app. This is about honesty, being accountable, and appreciating that even small decisions and expenses define your money situation and mindset.

For the past few months, categorize expenses, including restaurants, clothes, home goods, grocery stores, coffee, etc.

See any problem areas? See if you can drill down further. For example, if you notice you're spending a lot on meals and drinks out (coffee, happy hour), categorize those expenses by: "workweek lunch," "takeout for family dinners," etc.

What do you see? What's behind those expenses? For example, if you're spending too much on weeknight takeout with the kids, you might be feeling guilty for working long hours—and then coming home to spend more time cooking instead of with the kids. Instead, can you find a way to make meal planning and prep a family activity? Or, if the kids are older than eight, assign them a meal to be prepared before you get home—or if you can easily afford all the restaurant food, then keep buying it and stop feeling guilty for not June Cleaver-ing every meal!

Tomorrow is about really making serious changes to your money habits. Such good stuff! Stay tuned and see you then.

---- ☆ ----

Money Is Easy

Hey, Mama!

How you doing? How does this money makeover feel so far? Hard? *Good.* That means that the work is happening!

Today's exercise is to streamline your money management. This will be an ongoing process, but chances are, that hard look at all your accounts made you realize you have way too many accounts, too much information, and general overwhelm. The fewer accounts you have to manage, the fewer pieces of information, the more likely you are to be engaged and successful with your money.

I thought I was very streamlined with my money management and told everyone I only had two credit cards: one for business, one for personal. I realized I actually had four: Costco and Gap cards. Last month, I stopped using both my personal and Gap card, and now use my Costco card for all personal expenses (as you know, Costco requires customers use their card, which happens to have great points).

The easier you make your money management, the less you have to think about the basics of paying bills, and the more energy and time you'll have to spend on making, investing, and growing your bottom line.

TODAY'S BATTLECRY

"Money is easy!"

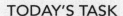

TODAY'S TASK

Simplify the crap out of your money management.

1. Set up auto-payment on every single account you can: rent, credit cards, car, insurance, utilities, phone. If you're not sure, call and ask or research online. Never miss another bill!

2. Set up paperless payments for everything. The environment thanks you, and vendors often give you a small discount.

3. Use as few credit and bank accounts as you can. Later, you and I will deal with debt, but until then, see if you can streamline your charging habits.

4. Change the payment dates on all your accounts to the same day—say, the first of each month. No more trying to remember when everything is due! Find ways to eliminate money tasks from your mind.

This process can take a little time, but it's so worth it. Invest an hour now, and get your life back!

What changes did you make to your money management? Share in Millionaire Single Moms (Facebook.com/groups/ millionairesinglemoms) on Facebook!

---　☆　---

DAY 6

Buy Nothing Month

Hey, Mama!

Wow, we are on Day 6 of the Kickass Single Mom Money Makeover. So far, you have made incredibly brave steps to changing your life forever.

Today is all about *not buying shit*. Our culture is hyperfocused on shopping for, consuming, and owning stuff. If you're not happy with your money situation, you're likely out of alignment with your values. If you always wish you had more or other things—a new wardrobe, a different/better/bigger house, a nicer car, better furniture—your thoughts and energy are engaged in a poverty mentality. You are focused on things, when deep down you know it's people and experiences that bring you joy and love. You become focused on what you *do not* have. You put little energy in being grateful and full with what you *do* have. Which, if you're reading this on a smartphone or laptop, then you already have *a lot*.

A personal shopping ban requires not just curbing the *buying*, but putting a stop to the *shopping*. No more browsing your favorite stores "just to look." No longer skimming online retailers "just to see what they have." No more careening from Target's grocery section to the home goods section "in case there are good deals."

The point is to recondition yourself from seeing shopping as an innocuous hobby, and instead focus on how much you do have and appreciate that it's more than enough.

Today I challenge you start a no shopping month. This means that you are very strict with yourself and aim to *buy nothing*. No new clothes. No toys or crap for your kids. Make a goal to eat through everything in your pantry, cupboards, fridge, freezer—including the granola bars in the glove compartment, but not necessarily all the booze in the liquor cabinet (I leave that to your discretion).

TODAY'S BATTLECRY

"I do not need new things. My life is full,
and I am so grateful!"

TODAY'S TASK

Start a daily gratitude practice. I have a notebook where I write down all the big and small things I am grateful for. Your practice may include prayer, mantra, or talking about gratitude with your kids. During a very dark time, a friend and I committed to a daily email exchange in which we each messaged each other what was wonderful in our lives, each and every morning. It may have saved me.

The second part of this task is *no more shopping for 30 days!* Easy, if you think about it.

———————— ☆ ————————

Set a Goal and Make a Budget

Hey, Mama!

Now that you have started crunching numbers, seeing how much you *actually* spend each month, and realizing how far you *actually* are from your goals, it's time to shake up your life.

That means two things:

1. Set a goal.

2. Take steps to get to that goal.

In other words: set a budget. Budgets aren't sexy and they're rarely fun, but they are empowering and necessary. Plus, you know you need one, and by simply doing this one thing, you relieve yourself of so much guilt and stress. Trust me, you will feel *incredible* after this task.

TODAY'S BATTLECRY

"I am a grown-ass woman and I am ready to set a goal and do the work it takes to get there!"

TODAY'S TASK

Write down your money goal. Here are some suggestions, but the goal is yours alone. The thing with goals is that they evolve and change as you move toward them. Perhaps you think that saving for a house right now is your priority, but as we talk about debt, emergency savings, and cash flow, that may change.

The trick is to stay focused yet flexible. Your money goal might include:

- ★ Pay off credit card debt
- ★ Maximize your 401(k) contribution
- ★ Save a $5,000 cash emergency fund
- ★ Buy a reliable used car in cash
- ★ Save $10,000 toward a home down payment

Write that goal down and post it where you can see it (bathroom mirror, by your desk at work, on the car dashboard). Get it up in your grill.

Next, make a Kickass Single Mom Budget:

1. Note your net income. This includes money that goes into your bank account, net of taxes, insurance, and other deductions that come from a job, side gigs, and child support and alimony. Write down the whole number, or use a simple Google Sheet. Tiller is also a great budgeting tool (Wealthysinglemommy.com/resources).

2. Write down your core expenses—what you are *actually* spending today. These include rent or mortgage, basic utilities, insurances, car pay-

ments, food, and taxes if you are self-employed and pay those directly.

3. Write down the rest of your expenses. Numbers two and three together should total your average monthly spending.

4. Write down your money goal. How much money does this goal require each month—whether to put toward debt, or save up?

5. Identify ways to slash your expenses. Start with the non-core expenses, and then move toward the core expenses (more on this tomorrow).

6. Automate your finances to meet that goal (I'll explain later!).

---------------------------- ☆ ----------------------------

DAY 8

Slash Expenses like Your (Financial) Life Depends on It!

I don't care what your money goal is, you very likely can stand to spend less than you are. You already committed to no shopping for a month. Now, here are ways that you can further cut your monthly and weekly expenses like a boss.

TODAY'S BATTLECRY

"The less I spend, the more I feel."

TODAY'S TASK

Take an hour and find ways to save on expenses.

Cable TV. I know, you love it. The kids love it. But this is serious business, and the whole family must get on board to make important changes. And it doesn't have to be forever. You can watch tons of stuff on your computer (or stream Netflix and Amazon videos to your TV, which is what I do). Also: read, play games, and other activities you keep telling yourself you'll do with the kids but don't get around to.

Gym membership. I really hope you're getting exercise and taking care of your body. But if you haven't been to the gym in more than two months, you must cancel that membership. Get real. Also, there are zillions of ways you can get and stay fit for free, including jogging, yoga, and training and aerobics at home.

Subscriptions. Go through all the subscription and automatic-renewal services on your bills. Upon close inspection, I realized I was paying for two monthly Netflix subscriptions. At $9.99 per month, that was costing me more than a hundred dollars per year. Sneaky on their part, lazy on mine! You may pay for membership to professional organizations that you're no longer interested in, or have access to publications or online services you don't use. Cancel, cancel, cancel.

Utilities. Get serious about using less electricity and gas:

- ★ Set the thermostat at a few degrees cooler in the winter.
- ★ Raise the AC a few degrees in the summer.
- ★ Keep blinds closed in the summer and unplug electronics when they're not in use.

Food. It can be very tempting for a busy, working single mom to splurge on restaurant food and prepared meals. Use these as special treats, or when a discount makes them a great deal. To save time and money:

★ Focus on cooking in bulk. I like to make a giant pot of stew, roast, or pasta sauce, eat a third that night, freeze a third, and eat the rest for lunches and dinner leftovers.

★ Avoid purchased lunches, and instead pack sandwiches and leftovers.

★ Remember: generic and bulk products tend to save you big bucks.

★ Eating healthy can be the least expensive way to eat. Replace meat with lentils and beans a few days per week. Focus on fresh fruits and vegetables. In many parts of the country, farm shares are very affordable ways to get local, fresh produce, while also supporting area farmers.

★ If your kids are age 8 or older, they can cook full meals by themselves. This cuts down on pressure for you to cook three full meals each day. The results are less exhaustion and stress on your part, a healthier bank account, and children on their way to a self-sufficient adulthood.

Holidays and birthdays. Christmas, Passover, birthdays, Valentine's Day—these special days can be especially stressful for single moms (they are for me). Co-parenting arrangements tend to implode during these events, and special times can feel especially empty without another parent to share them. The financial stress can make them anxiety-ridden for everyone involved. It's no wonder that overspending plagues the holidays—and single moms are especially vulnerable. To tackle this financial landmine:

★ Set a budget in August for the holidays.

★ Stick to it.

★ Establish in January a budget for each family member's birthday celebration and gift.

★ Focus on activities instead of things. Instead of toys, make part of the Christmas gift a family trip to the water park in the spring or a favorite museum (especially if you were planning to go to these places anyway). Studies find that experiences bring more and lasting enjoyment than things.

Insurance. Call your auto insurer and ask about lowering your rate:

★ Inquire about bundling your car, life, and homeowners policies for a discount.

★ If you own an older car, don't carry more than your state minimum, and note if you drive fewer than ten thousand miles per year, which could mean savings.

★ Research other car insurance policies. Especially if you are a longtime customer, your insurer is likely to give you a competitive rate—but you have to call and ask!

Phone. If you have a landline and a cell phone, cancel the landline. Then call your phone carrier and ask them to analyze your usage and suggest a more affordable plan. I did this and saved twenty dollars per month, effective immediately!

Did you find some hidden savings? Share your tips with us in Millionaire Single Moms (Facebook.com/groups/millionairesinglemoms).

-- ☆ --

DAY 9

Get Your Kids on Board!

Today's mission is fun and easy: talk to your kids about your money goals, and make them a *family goal*.

I don't care how old your kids are, it's your job to teach them about money and to have a positive, healthy relationship with personal finance. I know that might sound really hard if you're working through your own issues around money, but this is such an important part of your journey.

When you tell your child that as a family, you have created a money goal and explain what you will all do together to reach that goal, so many positive things are happening:

★ You hold yourself accountable.

★ You are transparent and honest about money, which likely is not usually 100 percent the case if you have money issues.

★ Break the cycle of money taboo!

★ You take a step in financial education for your kids, which is something you know you should do (thereby resolving some guilt).

★ You connect deeply with your kids, because you are now all working as a team toward something positive.

TODAY'S BATTLECRY

"I am the single most powerful source of financial information and habit-building for my kids. I have a moral obligation to be the best money management role model for everyone who is watching—especially my children!"

TODAY'S TASK

Create a plan to communicate your new financial goals with your kids.

The key here is to be honest and specific. Tell your kids: "It is important that we live within our income, live frugally, and appreciate what we have, which is a lot. That way, we will have money in the bank in case of an emergency, so we are secure in the future, and we can save for special things like vacations. To reach our savings/debt/car/home goal, we are going to make some changes. This includes . . ."

Tell them that you will eat out just once per month, will cut cable, and will stop hanging out at the mall on weekends. Keep track of your goal progress in a community place—like on a paper above the kitchen table.

Share how this is going with your family in Millionaire Single Moms (Facebook.com/groups/millionairesinglemoms).

---- ☆ ----

Declutter Your Home

Hey, Mama!

Today's task is both practical and spiritual.

I am a firm believer in living a simple, frugal life—a life full of gratitude for the things you do have, and surrounding yourself with items and people who fill you up and bring you joy and abundance in your emotions, health, experiences, and money.

Today's task is to cleanse your physical life of negative objects, with a special focus on negative past relationships (i.e., *the ex*). I have been separated/divorced for more than eight years, and I know this can be a long and hard process. For one, you may not be able to afford to replace all the furniture/dishes/clothes that have memories and emotions attached to past, negative people and experiences. In that case, today's exercise is designed to be a starting point, an opportunity to map out a long-term plan to renovate your possessions and life.

Plus, it's a big task! After years of systematic purges, I still occasionally come across a memento or household item that floods me with bad memories about my ex-husband. Case in point: in cleaning out the above-the-fridge cupboard, I found one of those big plastic Tupperware containers designed for cereal, which was the source of so much domestic contention when I was married. Stupid, but true. Needless to say: buh-bye, stupid Tupperware container!

When you rid your physical space of things that hold negative feelings and memories, you make room for positive experiences and feelings—like the feeling of having a shit-ton of money. Those items, big and small, help you let go of old ideas about who you used to think you were, and what you used to believe you were capable of, and makes room for a new, better, and more abundantly joyful you. Today's exercise will free your energy to attract all kinds of good things, money being just one of them: better relationships with your kids/friends/family, a new girlfriend/boyfriend, new work opportunities, travel—you name it.

Trust me on this. It may be hard at first, but you really just have to get rid of everything that you don't love or use.

TODAY'S BATTLECRY

"My surroundings reflect my self-identity.
I am in control of both."

Say it loud, and say it proud!

TODAY'S TASK

Identify one spot in your house that you dread dealing with the most. Perhaps a closet full of photos from your marriage, a garage shelf loaded with your ex's crap, a closet full of clothes that don't fit/are out of style from a time in your life that you senselessly pine for. Take an hour and tackle that spot. Be ruth-less. Brutal. Throw out everything and anything you absolutely have not used in the past month. Give it away or throw it away.

Sit for a moment when this is done (completely done—the crap at Goodwill or in the town dump). How do you feel? Pretty awesome, right?

Then, identify the next spot for tomorrow. Repeat. Repeat again.

Sometimes you can make cash by selling your old stuff. Thredup (Wealthysinglemommy.com/resources) is great for used clothes, and Craigslist for furniture, tools, appliances, and sports equipment. Decluttr (Wealthysinglemommy.com/resources) is my favorite for electronics, smartphones, cell phones, books, video games, DVDs, and CDs.

Related reading: "How to sell your engagement ring after divorce" (Wealthysinglemommy.com/resources)

What did you get rid of? How did it feel? Share your experience with us in Millionaire Single Moms (Facebook. com/groups/millionairesinglemoms).

—————————— ☆ ——————————

DAY 11

Can You *Really* Afford Your Home?

Hey, Mama!

You have your budget, and you have your goal. Today, I want you to take a very hard look at your housing situation. As your money situation stands *today,* is your current home *really* your best option?

One of the biggest mistakes I see single moms make is financially struggling to stay in a home they cannot easily afford. Whether you go into debt each month to make rent or mortgage, or constantly stress and put all kinds of negative energy into the universe just to make ends meet, this is a bad personal and financial decision.

I hear moms tell me the following reasons for staying in homes they can't afford:

> *"I love this house."*

> *"I want to keep the kids in a good school district."*

> *"Selling this house would be a public sign of failure. I don't want my neighbors and friends to know how broke I am."*

> *"This was the house I was supposed to grow old in with my 'whole' family. It's not fair that I have to move just because he had an affair and decided to get divorced."*

> *"I can barely make rent, but when I go to court and force my ex to pay more alimony/child support (or when I get my business off the ground/get that promotion), then it will be better."*

Here are the facts about what home you can afford:

1. What is the monthly cost to own or rent that does not stress you out? That is the home you need to live in right now. You can upgrade in the future when your finances are in a different spot. But perpetuating a lifestyle you cannot afford is living a lie. Nothing good comes of lies.

2. All those positive reasons for staying put are overshadowed by a nagging stress or outright panic for not being able to afford it. Again, when you are stressed about money, you are a stressed-out mom, you make decisions from a place of fear and frenzy, and you don't live up to your potential as a woman. You attract the wrong guys. You consider partnering with a man for financial reasons. You make money and career decisions based on fear.

This is one of my favorite passages from *The Kickass Single Mom:*

> *Ohio mom Wendy, together with her teenage daughters, moved out of a four-thousand-square-foot spread with five bedrooms and four bathrooms and into a three-bedroom, one-bath rental that was one-third the size. She took very few things from her previous home, which had been largely decorated with gifts and heirlooms from her ex-husband's parents.*
>
> *"Starting from nothing was daunting, but it was also completely liberating. I didn't have to ask anyone else their opinion. My choices were mine, and mine alone. It was a huge adjustment*

for my kids moving from a fancier home into a quite spare rental house. But it was a very valuable lesson in what actually makes a home: people, feelings, and memories, and not granite countertops and spiffy bathrooms.

"A year ago, I purchased a home just a few blocks from our rental house. We had grown to love our neighborhood and neighbors. Our new home is still small, and we still have only one bathroom, but the girls now regard this as their home. Their dad is now under contract with his latest girlfriend on a six-bedroom, five-bath stately Tudor on a very fancy street about a mile from us. The contrast between my house and that house could not be greater. And though I know we would all like more bathroom space, I have no doubt that this will continue to feel like my kids' home, however spacious and upscale his new digs are."

TODAY'S BATTLECRY

"I deserve to live in a home I can easily afford.
Today."

TODAY'S TASK

Get real about whether you can afford your current
home. You know the answer already. Make a plan.
This might include calling a mortgage broker, a real
estate agent, an apartment broker, or committing an
evening to culling the local rental ads.

Useful tool: The New York Times 'Rent or Buy?' calculator (Wealthysinglemommy.com/resources). Remember:
home ownership can be wonderful, but it's not
always right for everyone, all the time. Plenty of

> wealthy, successful, financially wise people chose to rent their homes.

Share your experience with us in Millionaire Single Moms (Facebook.com/groups/millionairesinglemoms).

☆

What's Your Credit Score?

Hey, Mama!

Today starts the debt-destroyer part of this challenge, and *it is going to be grooooood.*

If you are like most Americans, you have consumer debt: credit cards, medical debt, student loans, a car payment. Just because debt is so common doesn't mean it's not destructive. When you owe others money, they own you. Even if the interest rates are low and your credit score is solid, debt still erodes your life. When you're focused on paying back debt, your work, energy, and thoughts are focused on a *negative*—not on *building* wealth, assets, or a positive life.

If you are drowning in debt, you likely find it hard to

make payments on time, max out your limits, and other habits that result in a low credit score. When your credit score is low, you have fewer options: it's harder to get a mortgage or lease, trickier to start your dream business, and more difficult to buy or lease a new car when your old one dies. You deserve to have all the choices in the world. Your money situation can be a prison of few options, or a bountiful smorgasbord of choice and freedom. You deserve choice and freedom. Choice is power.

The first step is to retrieve your credit score and report. If your score is low, you likely have avoided your credit. This means that getting your score is that much more important. By doing so, you're telling the universe you're ready for change! In this case, that change means taking steps to boost your credit score and clean up your credit history.

TODAY'S BATTLECRY

"I am ready to take every necessary step to build my financial security and my family's future—no matter how uncomfortable or painful!"

TODAY'S TASK

Get your credit score. You can get your score and report totally free at Credit Sesame (Wealthysingle-mommy.com/resources).

I like Credit Sesame because it provides a *free* credit report, credit score, identity protection, and credit monitoring—totally free, no asking for your credit card number, "free" trials, or other baloney.

If you're looking to buy a home or a car, or get the very best rates on a credit card (0 percent) or business loan, a lender will look for a good credit rating. Here's the breakdown:

- ★ Excellent Credit: 750+
- ★ Good Credit: 700–749
- ★ Fair Credit: 650–699
- ★ Poor Credit: 600–649
- ★ Bad Credit: below 600

Tomorrow is all about making a plan to improve your credit score and history.

How did that feel? Bloody painful? Exhilarating? Share your experience with us in Millionaire Single Moms (Facebook. com/groups/millionairesinglemoms).

---- ☆ ----

DAY 13

Boost Your Credit Score

Hey, Mama!

Wow! We are almost halfway through the Kickass Single Mom 30-Day Money Makeover! I am *so proud* of you for getting this far. It's a lot of work, I know. You have to face issues and habits you'd rather avoid. All normal. So human. You are doing the hard work. Only good things come from facing the truth and taking steps for positive change. Have you slacked on your steps? No prob. Regroup and start again. All good, keep going!

Today, you will take your first steps in repairing your credit report and boosting your credit score.

TODAY'S BATTLECRY

"My credit score is important, and I am committed to facing my past mistakes and making changes so my credit report reflects my positive financial future."

TODAY'S TASK

Credit scores can seem complicated and intimidating, but achieving a score above 700 is actually simpler than you might think. Below, I outline a simple system for boosting your credit score by at least 100 points over a year—and at least 50 points within a month. The process takes patience, time, and diligence.

1. Pull up your credit report. A credit report is a list of all your loans and payment information. Get a report at Experian (Wealthysinglemommy. com/resources).

2. Clean up errors on your report. By law, you are entitled to have any obsolete, outdated, or erroneous errors removed. To do so, contact (in writing and sent by certified mail) the reporting credit bureau with documentation about why the item is wrong. By law, they have to remove these errors within 30 days of confirming your complaint is valid.

   Removing credit report errors is 100 percent doable and within your legal rights. That said, there are also some really great and legit tools where, for a modest fee, you can get some support. One is paying to help clean up errors on your credit history, like old errors that should have been removed by now, debts that your divorce decree specifies is the responsibility of your ex, debts that do not belong to you, or debts reported multiple times. Lexington Law (Wealthysinglemommy.com/resources) is an excellent service in this industry (there are a lot of very shady ones) and can make a lot of sense if you need to clean up your credit history ASAP, or simply want to outsource this task.

3. Commit to your debt payoff plan, as before.

4. Focus on paying off smaller balances. This is great for a quick credit score boost. If you have, say, $100 on a credit card, compared with $3,000 on a student loan account, paying off the smaller sum signals to the credit bureaus that you are tackling debt.

5. Self Lender (Wealthysinglemommy.com/resources) is another high-quality credit-boosting service that is unique. Self Lender offers a special type of loan called a credit-builder account—an installment loan that's secured by a Certificate of Deposit. Once your credit-builder loan account is approved, you'll be given a small loan to repay with the CD as collateral for the loan. At the end of the term, you will have paid back the loan with a reasonable interest rate, boosted your credit score, and landed with a savings account.

---- ☆ ----

DAY 14

Be Honest:
How Much Debt Do You Have?

Hey, Mama!

So now that you have your credit score, and you can see all your debt in one place, it's time to make a plan for getting rid of that shizzle!

1. Get real with your debt total. Look at those numbers on Personal Capital (Wealthysinglemommy.com/resources). Alternatively, collect statements for each and every one of your debts:

    ★ Credit cards

    ★ Medical bills

★ Student loans

★ Car note

★ Mortgage

★ Home equity line

★ Personal loans from your parents or cousin

★ Back taxes

★ Loans against your 401(k) or pension

Lay these out on the kitchen table. In paper. Feel them in your hands. Look them in the eye. I'm talking 100 percent transparency.

2. Create a list of all your debt, including interest rates, monthly minimum payments, and any deadlines—such as when promotion rates expire.

TODAY'S BATTLECRY

"When I owe others money, I lose power.
I am powerful, and my money reflects that."

Remember to say it *out loud*!

TODAY'S TASK

Stare at those debt numbers. Really hard. Do not look away. *Face the numbers.*

Related reading (Wealthysinglemommy.com/resources):

★ How single moms can pay off debt for good in 14 easy steps

★ A very awesome way to boost your credit score quickly while also creating a savings account

★ Should you pay for credit repair?

DAY 15

A Debt-Destroyer Plan That Works

Hey, Mama!

Now that you know what's what with your debt, it's time to make a monthly budget and figure out how much you can afford to pay toward your debt.

After you have cut out all those extra expenses, stopped shopping, and taken steps to live that elegantly simple life, how much extra do you have each month to devote to getting rid of debt?

Write that number down. That is the minimum you will devote to paying off debt each month.

Next, decide: Debt Avalanche or Debt Snowball? These terms are lingo for the two main methods for paying off debt.

★ Debt Snowball: Pay off credit cards or loans with the lowest balances first. The advantage is that you get the psychological and emotional thrill of paying off accounts quickly.

★ Debt Avalanche: Pay off accounts with the highest interest rates first. The big perk of this method is that you save more money by depleting high-interest debt sooner.

TODAY'S BATTLECRY

"I am committed to living debt-free. I am willing to do what it takes to pay off debt, and stay that way!"

TODAY'S TASK

Log into your debt accounts and make changes to reflect your decision. That means if you committed to the Debt Avalanche, and $800 per month more to pay toward your debt, identify the credit card or other debt with the highest interest rate and increase the monthly payment to that card to $800.

DAY 16

Negotiate Better Debt Rates

Hey, Mama!

Perhaps you are one of the very few Americans without consumer debt—no credit card balance, car note, student debt, outstanding medical bills, or money you owe your loved ones.

If so, *good for you, mama*!

For everyone else, here's some good news: you can usually negotiate your credit terms for a better rate.

First, see if you qualify for a 0 percent balance transfer. This post on MagnifyMoney (Wealthysinglemommy.com/resources) is a good place to start. This is a *great* way to pay off debt and save a lot of money on interest along the way. It only works if you are very organized, read all the fine print, and make sure you pay the premiums on time, and either pay off the balance or transfer the balance before the end of the promotion period.

Another way to get a better rate on your card is to call your current company and simply ask for a better rate. First, see what you qualify for on a site like Gobankingrates.com. Here's a script to help you:

> *"Hi, as you can see, I am a longtime cardholder and I love using your product. I am committed to paying off my debt and improving my credit history, and I'd love to stay with you. However, I need a better rate on my balance. Based on my research, I can get a [insert honest quote you received from another card] rate. Can you match it or do better?"*

TODAY'S BATTLECRY

"When I ask for what I want, with a sincere desire to make my life better in a meaningful way, I usually get it right away, and I always get it eventually."

TODAY'S TASK

Read this post: How single moms can pay off debt for good in 14 easy steps (Wealthysinglemommy. com/resources) for steps on how to negotiate medical bills, student loans, and other debt.

---- ☆ ----

Build That Emergency Savings Already

Hey, Mama!

Part of being wealthy is dealing with shame around being a financial hot mess. I have certainly been there: living paycheck-to-paycheck, no emergency savings, a credit card balance, car note, student loan, and a big fat $0 in retirement accounts.

Not a good look!

Before I could change that ugly scene, I had to be honest with myself about a) what a mess I was, b) how I got into that mess, and c) how to get out of it by making a plan that worked for me.

One of the most powerful tools in my financial arsenal actually has one of the *lowest* balances. That is my emergency savings fund. I like to keep around three months of business and personal expenses in a separate savings account that is *not* connected to my checking accounts or credit cards. This chunk of money sits there, in conservative investments, and does two things for me:

1. Serves as an actual safety net in the event that I have a medical emergency, a home or car repair pops up, my business unceremoniously tanks, or Armageddon hits.

2. In the more likely event none of those things happen, I walk around God's green earth with a bounce in my step thanks to the confidence that I am not SOL. The confidence and void of financial fear is actually the most powerful part of my entire financial portfolio, even though the dollars sum is but a small percentage of the rest of my assets. This account helps me make good, sound financial and business decisions every day, because those decisions are made from a place of confidence, not fear.

TODAY'S BATTLECRY

"I deserve to feel financially secure
every day, all the time."

TODAY'S TASK

If you have not set up an emergency fund, take that first step today. Three months' worth of expenses is a great goal, but if you are at $0, start with the goal of $1,000 and build from there.

This fund should *not* be at the same bank as your checking account (so that it's harder to toss money back and forth in the event you find a great vacation deal on TravelZoo). It should also be invested in a low-risk account.

Here are two places I highly recommend you can open a savings account:

1. Find a good, old-fashioned account from this list of the best online savings accounts (Wealthysinglemommy.com/resources).

2. Ellevest is a woman-focused investing platform that has financial plans to help you reach your goals—including a strategy for building emergency savings.

Did you open a new savings account? How did it make you feel? Write down that feeling, because it is special and important—no matter how small the deposit. Taking this step is forward, positive momentum. *Huge!*

DAY 18

Get Started Investing

Hey, Mama!

I am on a personal mission to get women to save and invest more. According to some fascinating studies I've read, women are actually *better* at investing than men, but they save and invest far too little, too infrequently, which puts us at a huge disadvantage. The *wealth gap* is a terrible issue, as women have far less invested and saved than men, and we need those long-term assets even more than dudes since:

a) women will live longer, on average,

b) women are disproportionately more likely to be responsible for children and aging relatives, and

    c) statistically women earn less during our careers (damn you, pay gap!), and therefore receive less from Social Security.

Plus, we are better at investing, so we should just be investing and growing our money for the sake of the economy, gender equality, and national security—am I right?

It pisses me off to no end, and I am set on fixing this. That passion is the root of why I do this work with single moms and women everywhere.

But enough about me. On to *you* and *your money*, which must include investing for the long-term.

TODAY'S BATTLECRY

"I am in control of my financial future,
and I have the power to start investing today."

TODAY'S TASK

Read this post: "How to get started investing for women," which you can find at wealthysinglemommy.com/resources, and do what the post says!

Then, write down your experience. If you *do* have a great foundation to your retirement investments, articulate in writing how this makes you *feel*. If you're just starting out, or worry you have a lot of catching up to do when it comes to your retirement savings, write that down too. It's so powerful to articulate your fears and joys. Honesty is required for change.

Avoid These Common Investing Mistakes

Hey, Mama!

Yesterday, you learned about investing basics, all of which are outlined in an easy, step-by-step guide in this post: How to get started investing for women (Wealthysinglemommy. com/resources).

There are some investing mistakes that women in particular make—some of them are strategic mistakes, and others are internal mindsets that hold them back.

Here are some of the most common investing mistakes women—and single moms in particular—are prone to make:

1. Believe that money is better spent on our kids or families than our futures.

In a survey by financial services giant Allianz, nearly half of single moms say that saving for their children's education is their No. 1 greatest motivation for developing a long-term financial plan—above saving for retirement. Compare that with just 26 percent of other modern families who say the same, according to the Allianz survey. The best gift you can give your children now is your own financial security. This models great money lessons for your children now and ensures that you'll be less likely to be a burden on your children in the future. A parent's own financial freedom is such a blessing for any child, of any age. Meanwhile, keep in mind that there are countless opportunities for your kids to finance college.

2. Believe a man is a financial plan.

Maybe one day you'll couple with a man who has more money than you and is willing to share his money, and that will bolster your financial security. Even then, you need to take care of yourself and your finances. You still need to build your wealth as an independent, adult woman, because you *are,* and you *can.*

3. Fail to diversify.

The best indicator of high return on your investments is taking calculated risks and diversifying. That means that you own lots of different types of investments, across all types of sectors. As a nonfinancial professional, it can be debilitating to try to figure out how to do that. The best way is through buying mutual funds. That might sound complicated and confusing, and *it is.* Don't try to do this on your own. In this post (Wealthysinglemommy.com/resources), I explain how very smart, successful women are often embarrassed by how confused they are by investing. I explain how to find affordable, secure ways to grow your money.

4. "I don't invest in the market because I don't understand stocks and bonds."

You know what? I don't deeply understand stocks and bonds, either. You know what else I don't deeply understand? The tax code, so I hire an accountant. I don't deeply understand how to grow natural fibers, make cloth, and sew, so I shop for my clothes and linens. I'm not much of one to understand how digital electronics function, much less are manufactured, so I leave that jazz to Apple, Sony, and Bose. You are not Ma Ingalls on the prairie where everything is DIY. You live in the twenty-first century where almost everything in your life is outsourced to someone who knows how to do it better. Your investments are no exception. Pay a low fee for a mutual fund, which means you pay a small amount of money to an expert who creates a financial product—a fund—that is diversified and will likely help you meet your goals.

5. "My home is my retirement."

First, read #3 on this list of mistakes. A house is sometimes an investment, but if that is all you have for retirement, it could not be less diversified—it is parking all of your future in one ZIP code, in one property, in one market. Far, far too much risk to be even close to reasonable. Plus, you need to live somewhere. Let's say that when you are 67 you decide to retire, but that year, the U.S. real estate market tanks and your town floods. Everyone in your neighborhood is also trying to sell their soggy homes, with the intention of then becoming a renter. House prices plummet, while rental prices skyrocket. Even if you do sell your home for a modest sum, that will not go far. Stay or go, you are stuck.

That's why you need to invest in lots of different things, all with different risks, different markets, locations, industries.

The cheapest, easiest way to do that is by choosing the right funds.

TODAY'S BATTLECRY

"I am humble, and by being humble, I am powerful. I will admit to what I do not know and understand, and will seek and accept help. That is how I grow more powerful and secure."

TODAY'S TASK

Write down three or more things about investing that you don't understand or find intimidating. This might be a word, tool, or process that you feel like you should know but don't. Commit to spending an hour researching these terms.

Then, reach out for further support in Millionaire Single Moms. We are right here with you!

———————— ☆ ————————

DAY 20

Who Holds You Accountable?

Hey, Mama!

Over the past few weeks, we've been talking about budgeting, saving, investing, and debt. We also talked a lot about money mindsets. Negative money mindsets plague everyone, but the brand of negative self-talk when it comes to single moms is unique.

One of my own personal growth breakthroughs in my life—including around money—is learning to ask for help. As a child, I was taught to ignore any emotions perceived as "bad" (feeling sad, angry, jealous, bitter, heartbroken). I also felt as a child I couldn't count on people. These two things went hand in hand. Not only did my parents let me down in important ways, but also I was taught to deny my feelings. **How can you even think to ask for help if you aren't allowed to recognize you need it?**

As an adult, I am so grateful to realize that *everyone* needs help. Everyone experiences every emotion, and humans are limited and fallible. It's those limitations that drive us to seek help from others. That help may come in the form of logistical support, such as asking a neighbor to watch your kids when you have a really hot date and your ex flakes on his visit. Or it may be emotional support, such as asking for encouragement when you feel guilty for having insanely audacious dreams, or as if you will never meet your money goals. It's that interdependence of people that creates social and emotional connections, communities, tribes, relationships, and families—the very connections that are among the most important experiences a human can have.

In other words, needing help fosters the very relationships that you and I and the Pope and Oprah and everyone else seek out the most.

By taking this money challenge, you have consciously sought out a very big shift in your life. This is hard. This is *very hard*. This kind of shift requires not simple budgeting strategies. That's easy, and that doesn't work to make significant change in your life. To change your money situation—to have more money, to feel abundant, to be powerful and in control of your finances—requires a spiritual, emotional, and social change. That is *hard*. This work requires support.

TODAY'S BATTLECRY— REMEMBER TO SAY IT OUT LOUD!

"I am not alone. I have all the support and love I need to make positive change in my life, and the lives of my children. All I have to do is ask for the support I need and be ready to receive it."

TODAY'S TASK

Identify an area of your money mindset that's challenging, and seek out the support you need. Perhaps this means asking for help and care from your accountability partner, your romantic partner, a good friend, colleague, or family member. Tell them what you need. Receive it. Feel lost for a person in your life? Head right now to our closed Facebook group Millionaire Single Moms (Facebook.com/groups/millionairesinglemoms). We are your tribe!

———————— ☆ ————————

DAY 21

Tough Talk about
Child Support and Alimony

Hey, Mama!

The Kickass Single Mom Money Makeover is not a generic money exercise. This is specifically for *single moms.* For most single moms, your kids have a father in the picture in some form. Child support and/or alimony are likely part of your single mom story—especially if you don't get all you feel you are owed.

My goal for all single moms, everywhere, is to enjoy the freedom, independence, and pride of building a life without depending on a man for child support or alimony. Note: child support is monthly payments to maintain your home and food, while *extras* are out-of-pocket expenses that parents can and should split in a fair way (insurance, health care, childcare, and extracurriculars). Alimony is designed to keep women in "lifestyles to which they are accustomed," supported by men they are no longer in romantic relationships with.

Money very, very rarely does not cause conflict between divorced or separated partners, which destroys the possibility of healthy co-parenting. Also, any negative energy about money with your kids' dad is just that: negative energy.

From *The Kickass Single Mom* book:

> *The indisputable argument against any type of support is that it's irresponsible to build a life around income you have no control over. Your kids' dad could lose his job, die, become disabled, chose a lower-paying career, see his business tank, hide all of his income offshore, get busted for cooking meth in a trailer in the middle of the New Mexico desert and be sentenced to the can, or simply go MIA. You have no control over that, and if you depend on his income, you live in fear every single day that it will go away. That is a terrifying, exhausting way to live. Shift that toxic, fearful energy into your own income and*

career, which you do have control over, and watch your life change forever and for the better.

The cost of depending on child support is bigger than this. If you take and depend on that income, you are less likely to launch the business of your dreams, act on your urge to go for a big promotion, or go back to school to pursue a new career. After all, you know that the more you earn, the less he will have to pay in both support and extras. While you may tell yourself that money is going into a savings account for the kids, it is very difficult to mentally shut it out of your monthly budget, especially if it is a significant sum. The more you depend on income from your ex, the more power you give him over you, and the less ownership you take for your own success.

As for alimony, here's what I wrote in *The Kickass Single Mom:*

Alimony reform is under way in just about every state in the country. In most states, lifetime alimony is now a thing of the past, and the sums and rules granted to payees grow stricter all the time. Policy makers and judges enforcing the law have seen for years how alimony stifles divorced couples' ability to effectively co-parent by creating tension between exes, and prevents the lesser-earning spouse (nearly always the wife) from moving forward with her life. Alimony, judges know, disincentivizes both the paying and receiving spouses from building their careers, and results in years of expensive and bitter appeals in court. In fact, alimony is the number-one most appealed issue in divorce courts.

Even more than the realities of divorce court rulings, the real reason for eliminating alimony from your financial plan is that it holds you back in every part of your life. There are few things in this life that are as delicious as assessing your home, your bank account, and the career and business you built, wrapping your arms around yourself, and saying: "I did this. I did all of this! And if I can do this, just look what else I can do in this world!" You cannot live your full potential as a mother or person if you choose to be financially dependent on anyone else, much less a man with whom you are no longer financially or romantically entangled.

TODAY'S BATTLECRY—
REMEMBER TO SAY IT OUT LOUD!

"I deserve to feel the amazing, unique power of being completely financially independent—independent from debt, from reliance on my parents, and from a man or government programs for my future."

TODAY'S TASK

First, be honest with yourself. How do you feel when you take money from your kids' dad? How do you feel about fighting with him over money? Write down any downsides of that money exchange—or fighting for money. Write down all the energy and time you spend getting that money and being mad about not getting more. Do these arguments bring you back to bad times during the relationship? Does it make it harder to move on and heal? Finally, do you ever under-earn or manipulate your income to qualify for more alimony or child support? Be honest: How does that make you feel?

Next, make a plan to stop relying on child support and alimony. I appreciate that you may receive it now and may very much feel that you need it. Also, you may not receive money you are owed but spend a lot of time, energy, and even money fighting for it or being angry about it.

Take a breath.

Consider this: you deserve not to feel angry or spend negative energy on getting that money out of a man. You cannot change him. You can change yourself. You can, right here today, make a plan to let go of any sense of entitlement to his money—no matter how much you are legally or even ethically owed it. Today, recognize that you have the power to build whatever lifestyle *you* want to become accustomed to! You deserve all the financial security in the world, and to never be limited by another person—especially one who you are no longer in a romantic relationship with!

In a few days, we will start exploring how you can *make* more money and *grow* your bottom line, career, and income. Think about that as you sit with today's task on your relationship with alimony or child support.

☆

Focus on How Freaking Abundant Your Life Is

Hey, Mama!

When I first became a single mom, I was so terrified. I was obsessed with the quality of life I *used* to have with my (ex) husband. I was always watching what my married friends wore, new things they bought for their home, and (the worst of all) the vacations they boasted about on social media.

First of all, just because people have fancy things or trips does not mean that they can afford them—after all, so many people purchase all this stuff, but most people also have debt and no savings!

But the real point of today's task is to help you focus on how much you *do* have and recognize how absolutely abundant your life already is. When you focus on what you do have—and not on what you don't have, or covet—**your energy refocuses away from a poverty mentality, and into an abundance mentality**.

TODAY'S BATTLECRY— REMEMBER TO SAY IT OUT LOUD!

"By the mere fact that I can read this challenge on an electronic device attached to the internet in a warm, safe place means that I am wealthier than 99 percent of the people on this planet. I am so unbelievably grateful for everything I have, and I have the power to create even more abundance—as much as I desire. In fact, it's embarrassing how abundant my life is!"

TODAY'S TASK

Get out a pen and paper, baby. You are going to write. Write down every single thing and feeling and fact you are grateful for. For your health. Health of loved ones. Abundance of food at your disposal. A job. Nice people in your life. That you live in a time and place of unprecedented opportunities for women. Peacetime. That dime you found on the sidewalk. That you didn't get a parking ticket even though you should have (on my personal list today!). That hug your kid gave you this morning, or that your BFF made you crack up. That you never worry about clean water coming out of the faucet when you turn it on. Wine. Magnums. That you are loved. For the internet that connects you with amazing people and ideas and community and opportunities all around the world.

I could go on for days. You can too.

This exercise is so sosososososososo powerful. It feels so fucking good. Do it every day. Your life will change.

---- ☆ ----

Take a Cold, Hard Look at Your Career

Hey, Mama!

Throughout my work, I constantly discourage women from anything that keeps them thinking small. Go big, or go home. You only have so many hours in the day, only so many kilowatts of energy, only so many years on this planet. Do you want to focus on clipping coupons, arguing with your ex over money, or slogging away at a *meh* job that pays the bills? Or, do you want to build an incredible life where your energy is spent creating meaningful work that helps others, generates tons of money, and sets an incredible example for your kids and everyone else around you?

I thought so.

When it comes to money, it can be an easy crutch to focus on *saving* money by cutting costs and bargain shopping. These things are so important, but you can only cut so much. However, when you focus on *earning,* the sky's the limit! Plus, when you focus on building a career or a business, there are so many residual positives. You bring joy and productivity into your life. You effect the world in a positive way. You attract other joyful, successful people into your professional and personal (and romantic, trust me on this) lives. All of this growth is so good for you as a woman and a mother, and inspires others around you to live to a higher standard.

In other words, *when you succeed, you give others permission to succeed.*

Your children. Your neighbors and colleagues. Your friends. This is activism. It is important and powerful.

Today's task might be really easy for you—you may currently be building your next career chapter and are cruising! However, you might join many other women who are frustrated, scared, unsure, or confused about where they are on their career journey.

TODAY'S BATTLECRY— REMEMBER TO SAY IT OUT LOUD!

"I have amazing gifts and talents that I deserve to be paid a lot of money for. I deserve to wake up excited, proud, and positive about my career! Loving my work is not a luxury allocated for a special few. I deserve both money and joyful work."

TODAY'S TASK

Get really real with yourself about your career. Sit down and get in touch with how you *feel* about your job, your income, your daily schedule, and the people you spend time with at work. Ask yourself:

★ Am I happy with my income?

★ Do I feel appreciated?

★ Is what I do each day in alignment with my values?

★ Do I respect the people I work for and with?

★ Does this work showcase my greatest talents and skills that I have to offer the world?

★ Do I like my job?

You may find this truth through meditation, prayer, hiking in the woods, exercising, sex, yoga, or before you fall asleep at night. This is an exercise in *feeling*, not thinking. Do not focus on rationalization, like, "I hate my job, but this work allows me to be there for my kids," or, "I am really bitter that I am not paid more, but my job is secure," or, "I am underpaid, overworked, and treated poorly—but not everyone can love their work and get paid a lot, ya know!"

This exercise may take some days and weeks to work on—I am constantly revising my relationship with my work and tweaking my business, art, and income goals as a result. Be gentle with yourself, but also brutally honest.

Remember: you love money! (You said that a few days ago.) Also: loving your work is not a treat, but something you deserve and can achieve.

Was today's task tricky? Share your feels in Millionaire Single Moms (Facebook.com/groups/millionairesinglemoms) on Facebook. We are your tribe!

Set a Big-Arse Career Goal

Hey, Mama!

Yesterday, you were assigned a frank look at how you *feel* about your career. What you do each day. How much you earn. The people you work with and for. The people or causes you serve. How these things align with your sense of joy, appreciation, values, and your healthy, awesome desire for a lot of money.

TODAY'S BATTLECRY—
REMEMBER TO SAY IT OUT LOUD!

"I am worthy of all the career
and financial success I desire."

TODAY'S TASK

Write down a big-arse, scary career goal. Here's my secret to achieving goals:

Step 1: Set a goal.

Step 2: Revise goal to make it so big and crazy it scares you.

For many years on January 1, I would set income and other goals for my business—and I would always blow that goal out of the water. I'd get so *pissed* at myself for not setting a bigger goal. If it doesn't make you uncomfortable, the goal is not worth making.

Step 3: Be really specific about what you want. "I want a big raise this year" is not enough. "I want to earn $20,000 more by Christmas, and to be in a new position where I am able to exercise my vision for my team" is specific.

Step 4: Be careful about who you share that goal with. I have a tight circle of accountability partners, mentors, and homegirls and homeboys who have my back. Others don't need to know about my goals. I don't welcome random energy into my circle. Gotta keep this sphere void of any toxic energy.

Step 5: Identify the intention behind the goal. Your objective must not include only money or a title or vanity metric (like attracting a certain number of Instagram followers, or making a bestseller list). The goal must include meaningful accomplishments, like serving others in a campaign you are passionate about, or jumping out of bed with excitement every (or, most!) morning, or being a positive role model to your children.

Also, I learned early on that money or titles are not enough. You must serve others. When you focus on how you can create positive change in the world and seek joy in your work, that's when you do your *best* work and have meaningful, impactful, and long-lasting success. Since we are so abundant, that is our obligation.

———————— ☆ ————————

DAY 25

Get That Raise You Deserve

Hey, Mama!

If you want to make more money, often that means *asking* for more money—whether by getting a different job with a higher salary, starting a business where you will set rates that will bring in more income, or by asking your current employer or clients for a raise. Better yet—tell your boss or client that your rate is going up!

In *Women Don't Ask: Negotiation and the Gender Divide* (Wealthysinglemommy.com/resources) by Linda Babcock and Sara Laschever, the authors show women negotiate *30 percent less often* than men and, when we do, we ask for *up to $16,000 less.*

Low confidence and lack of female role models in leadership

positions are to blame. I also argue women are taught that prioritizing money is unseemly and the equivalent to greedy. Eff that!

The net result? In 2015, the gender wage gap narrowed by just .4 of a percent. In fact, the pay gap "*has not shown a statistically significant annual increase since 2007*," according to the US Census Bureau!

TODAY'S BATTLECRY

"Upping my fee or asking for a raise
is business—not personal."

TODAY'S TASK

Commit to asking for that raise. Instructions below. You will learn:

1. The one mindset shift that will help you get over your fear of asking for a raise.

2. How to find out what you are worth.

3. How to ask for the damn raise already.

1. A Raise Is Business, Not Personal

The PayScale survey found employees avoid salary negotiation because they're worried about being fired or appearing too pushy (like women fear being called *bossy?*).

But a negotiation is not about whether people like each other; it's a conversation with the goal of coming to a mutual decision that benefits both parties. It can actually be a win-win situation if you bring up the pay scale in the right manner.

If you are paid fairly, you are more committed to your work and company. Your boss feels more confident that you will be a better employee and stay around longer. Bosses *hate* replacing workers. It's expensive and time-consuming.

Capitalize on that fear!

2. Do Your Salary Research

First, understand your value in the marketplace to see if there's really wiggle room, or if you're asking for a pay raise without a good reason.

Check sites like PayScale and CareerBuilder, look at comparable job postings, ask your colleagues, and inquire with industry associations and recruiters. Then, define your boss's and the company's greatest needs and challenges. Understand how your past performance and current skills address those pain points.

Whenever possible, quantify your success and put a number on it. Prove how your marketing efforts drove this much more traffic to the company's website, or that you exceeded sales goals, which meant X million dollars in more revenue for them.

If your firm's top priority is to grow a certain segment of their business, show how your deep contacts within the group have already led to the bottom line and can stand to contribute even more next year. Focus on the other party.

Also, consider timing. If it's been more than a year since your raise or hire, or evaluations are just several months away, now is a good time to approach the boss.

Most companies stipulate a certain sum of money for payroll, raises, and bonuses, and some of that can be decided based on performance reviews. That said, even if your colleagues warn you that a raise is not likely, consider going for it anyway. But if there have been massive layoffs or any other kind of financial crises, you probably won't gain anything from going for it.

3. Ask for That Raise!

Approach your boss about meeting to discuss your salary. Keep communication in line with your normal exchanges.

For example, if your boss is typically very direct, also be direct. If you have frank weekly lunch meetings, bring it up then. If you chat face-to-face throughout the day, it may seem unusually passive to suddenly approach them by email. Likewise, if you're on instant message throughout the workday, suddenly popping into their cubicle could be surprising.

Use this type of language to set up the meeting:

"Can we meet in the next week to discuss my compensation?"

During the meeting, keep the tone light, direct, and non-emotional (it's business, not personal!).

Arrive armed with documents backing your performance, but start with a verbal, top-line summary of your accomplishments, as well as any additional responsibilities you've taken on during your tenure.

Don't forget to position your case to appeal to their interests. And don't take for granted your boss is aware of all of your duties or successes. If your research indicates you're paid below market, mention that too. Here's a script:

"I believe my accomplishments deserve a salary of X based on what other positions are paying, and my successes for the company."

Bonus tip: Always Have a plan B

In the event you're turned down, ask about other benefits.

For example, see if your company pays a "spot bonus," a reward for a single project done well. Or counter with a more flexible work schedule, more vacation time, or increased training possibilities.

If you're finding difficulty in getting a raise in your current situation, consider looking for a new job. Some of the biggest pay raises typically come when workers switch companies.

———————— ☆ ————————

DAY 26

Network, Baby!

Hey, Mama!

Some really annoying life coach somewhere coined the phrase, "Your network is your net worth." I'm repeating it, because it's true.

A recent CareerXroads survey found that only 15 percent of jobs are landed by sending your résumé into the black hole that is job boards. The rest? *Networking.*

What is networking? Here are some examples of how I've gotten paying jobs via networking:

People I vaguely know on Facebook who vaguely know what I do for work reached out and asked if I was open to new work.

Random people who found me on LinkedIn, which I obsessively update and work.

A guy I chatted with once at the gym referred me to a client who hired me.

A mom of my kid's friend who noticed my email signature while we were sorting out a play date.

I went for lunch with an old friend and shared my goals with her. She said: "I know who you should talk to!" and introduced me via email to a friend who got me a job.

Colleagues I worked with a zillion years ago who, when I was in a pickle of my own at various times in my life, got a call or email or Facebook message from me saying, "Hey! I have an opening in my workflow. What are you working on that I can help with?"

Friends—intimate and otherwise—who got calls, emails, and LinkedIn messages from me saying, "A couple of my clients restructured and I'm looking for leads. Anyone you know looking for XYZ?"

OKCupid dates who were in my industry, or knew people who were in my industry, and needed my expertise and referred me.

Childhood friend I saw for the first time since high school at my twentieth high school reunion who offered to introduce me to his well-positioned uncle who lives in my city—an offer I accepted. (Key: if someone offers to help you with something you need help with [and sometimes when you don't], you must take it. Otherwise, you are telling the universe to go fuck itself. Don't do that.)

High school friend I bumped into at a wedding referred me to a friend of a friend who landed me an interview at *60 Minutes.*

My mom's friend.

Someone who turned me down for a job referred me to his ex-wife who hired me.

Walking my ass into businesses and introducing myself.

TODAY'S BATTLECRY

"The key to making my dreams come true is connecting with the right people. The universe will conspire to help me find those people."

TODAY'S TASK

First, dig into all the contacts you have and make a list of all of them: personal friends, colleagues, and acquaintances. Networking also means meeting new people. For the next week, contact at least 20 people every day. Every. Single. Day.

That is 100 people in one week. That sounds like a lot, but think about how many Facebook friends you have. How many email contacts, LinkedIn connections, Twitter followers, or Pinterest followers do you have? Many of these are people you actually know at least a little, if not a lot. Even the ones you have never chatted with—digitally or otherwise—are contacts.

These communications should very briefly outline to the other person:

1. Your goals

2. What you offer

3. Ask what you can do for them. As always in life, give as much as you can. It comes back around. Always. Say: "What are you working on that I can support?"

4. Listen. Yes, listen to their request and do your best to help. But also ask questions about what's going on at their company, their industry, what their predictions and experiences are. That's how you learn about opportunities that you may not have considered. Listening also gives you the chance to identify connections and opportunities for other people you know—which is the No. 1 best way to cultivate good career and money mojo. Plus, helping others feels awesome!

Part of setting these big goals is to jump-start your goal-making momentum. The more people you reach out to, the more feedback you'll get. The more positive reactions, introductions, and referrals you receive, the more positive you will feel about reaching your goals and getting that money rolling in!

For specific email and phone scripts to use when reaching out to contacts and making new contacts, check out *Make More Money Now* (Wealthysinglemommy.com/resources), my e-book course designed to help you get out of *stuck* and *broke* and into a *job* and making money *now*.

--- ☆ ---

DAY 27

Start That Side Gig

Hey, Mama!

One of the most incredible things about being a mom in this era is access to incredible technology. Not only does the internet connect you and me, as well as you and all the 13,000+ women in Millionaire Single Moms, but you can also meet thousands of men via dating sites, career opportunities via LinkedIn, job boards and networking sites, and two words: Amazon Prime.

Technology also means you have untold opportunities to create a business with little financial investment, from home, in your free time. A side gig is not only an incredible income opportunity, but it can also be very personally fulfilling, and is a great way to create security—after all, should your main job go away, you always have at least a little income coming in from your side hustle. In my case, my side gig—Wealthysinglemommy.com—turned into my full-time career and passion, and my income quadrupled when I stopped writing for clients in my freelance business, and instead chose to grow my media company serving single moms.

TODAY'S BATTLECRY

"Multiple streams of income are a great way to try a new field, have fun, and make my family more financially secure. I deserve it all!"

TODAY'S TASK

The opportunities for income on the side are endless. One of my favorite sites for flexible, work-at-home jobs is FlexJobs (Wealthysinglemommy.com/resources), which was started by a mom named Sara Sutton Fell, who was frustrated with the lack of resources like this.

Here are a couple articles to help you get started (Wealthy singlemommy.com/resources):

★ "Legit ways to make income right now"

★ "Top companies for a work-at-home job"

---------------------- ☆ ----------------------

DAY 28

Outsource Like a Mother

Hey, Mama!

Fact: ***No one has ever become wealthy without outsourcing.***

You cannot build a successful business by doing it all yourself. Eventually, you realize that you have special talents and you must hire others, or find technology, to take over tasks that you are either overqualified for, or otherwise are best performed by someone who does them better. This is also true if you are a professional, and for every single woman reading this book who runs a household.

Women are super-weird about outsourcing household tasks. They tell me, "Doing one's laundry is simply a part of life."

Or, "If my family heard I hired a housekeeper, they would think me a snob."

Or, "Cooking homemade meals for my family every day is simply what good mothers do."

Look, you already outsource nearly every task in your life. You don't wash your clothes on rocks in the river. You outsource laundry to sophisticated machines. You don't grow, harvest, preserve, and cook food over a wood stove. You buy food—probably plenty of pre-prepared and packaged food—at the store and make a meal out of it in your kitchen full of very advanced cooking tools and devices.

TODAY'S BATTLECRY

"No one has ever become wealthy without out-sourcing. I deserve to be wealthy, and I deserve to outsource. It's a no-brainer."

TODAY'S TASK

Identify three tasks in your home or business that you can outsource. Commit to using that extra time to build your income or to rejuvenate yourself so you can better serve your family, career, and community.

A few ideas to get you started:

★ Laundry

★ Meal prep

★ Chauffeuring kids to after-school activities

★ Housekeeping

★ Yard work

★ Pet care

★ Mundane work tasks that a junior person should do, such as scheduling or social media posting

★ Things in your side business that you can
do (say, basic web design or bookkeeping)
but would be much better performed by a
specialist

Then, outsource those things. BAM!

I know the pushback: *But, Emma—not everyone is a
wealthy single mommy! I can't afford to outsource!*

To this, I say: You have to take a risk with the
confidence that it will pay off. You invest money in
housekeeping now, that makes your week and life in-
finitely better. You have more time to build your side
gig, more energy for your kids, or better performance
at your full-time job. Extra hours to exercise, which
helps you look and feel incredible—sentiments that
trickle into the rest of your life.

The return on outsourcing may not be immediate,
but if used constructively and with gratitude, it will
change your life in dramatic ways.

---- ☆ ----

DAY 29

Smooch Yourself

Hey, Mama!

This is Day 29—you've almost completed this monster challenge. This is so incredible. No matter how much progress you made, no matter whether you tackled every single task, just taking a step on this journey is huge.

You recognized a need for change, *and took responsibility for that change.* All good things stem from the moment you decided to own responsibility for your success.

Today, your job is to take stock of how far you've come and where you are on your money mastery journey.

TODAY'S BATTLECRY

"No one is responsible for my financial well-being but me. I am in control of my financial future. I am powerful!"

TODAY'S TASK

Write down how far you have come in your money journey. Answer these questions:

1. What is the biggest mental or emotional road-block you recognized that was or is holding you back financially?

2. What have you done to overcome that mindset?

3. Do you check your Personal Capital account regularly? How about Ellevest? How does your savings account look (Wealthysinglemommy. com/resources)? Your credit score and debt pay-down plan? How do you feel about your financial snapshot?

4. How much have you reduced your monthly expenses? How have you done on your no-spend month and simple living plan?

5. What steps have you taken to get on track for retirement?

6. How do you feel about your new career path? What steps have you taken to boost your income and create a dream career?

7. Overall, how do you feel about this challenge? What was the hardest part? The most inspiring? What do you need help with next?

Now sit with what you wrote. Appreciate it all. The hard parts. The amazing parts. The times when you flaked out and did not complete a task. The spot where you maybe stopped altogether and did not move forward. This is all part of the process. You own this book now, and you can pick it up anytime you are ready. You can (and should!) repeat parts—including parts that you mastered.

No matter what, give yourself a hug. Whether that means a smile in the mirror, a congratulatory deep breath, or an actual physical hug. You did some important work here, and your life and family already benefit.

———————— ☆ ————————

DAY 30

The First Day
of the Rest of Your Life

Hey, Mama!

You did it. You completed the 30-Day Kickass Single Mom Money Makeover.

So huge.

I don't expect that in one month all your debt is paid off, you have a new job, a higher credit score, *and* a crystal-clear money mindset.

If you are a money mess, that was *years* in the making, and real, deep, positive change takes time. Hard work and time. Abundance also requires giving back. After all, if you are fortunate enough to have so much, it's your duty to give to others.

TODAY'S BATTLECRY

"I am committed to the long, hard work of taking ownership of my money. Every single day, I make the decision to stay the course to live a simple life full of gratitude and giving."

TODAY'S TASK

Commit to inspiring others to live abundant, financially sound lives full of meaningful work and a healthy relationship with money. You might:

1. Have a refreshingly open and honest money conversation with your friends. Break the taboo and share how much you earn, your debt situation, or how you feel about your retirement plans.

2. Encourage someone you know to ask for a much-earned raise or promotion, or to open their dream business.

3. Introduce someone without a financial compass to your favorite personal finance books, websites, or social channels.

4. Volunteer with young people, women in a shelter situation, English learners, or others who benefit from basic financial literacy.

5. Prioritize teaching your kids about money.

6. Initiate low-cost or free activities when you get together with your friends. They likely would love to save money, but are shy about being the first to ask to skip expensive restaurants or sports events.

7. Start a local investing club or a personal finance salon where you discuss money and support each other's goals.

For more details on how I went from a broke, in-debt single mom with babies to running a multiple-six-figure business from home, check out my number-one bestseller *The Kickass Single Mom* on Amazon (Wealthysinglemommy. com/resources).

Taking full control of your personal finances is a critical step to living your fullest life. Switching your thoughts and emotions around money from stress and panic to abundance, security, and joy is life-changing. You now have the time, energy, and bandwidth to create whatever life you care to dream up.

By simply taking this step and committing to this new life long-term, you are changing the world for your family, for other women and their families, and for all of us.

Mama, thank you for your work.

———————— ☆ ————————

SNEAK-PEEK OF MY UPCOMING BOOK:

WTF WEDNESDAYS:
SINGLE MOM Q&A ON
MONEY, SEX, PARENTING AND LIFE

For three years on Wealthysinglemommy.com, I ran a column, WTF Wednesdays, in which I answered reader questions about single-mom challenges. Moms loved it, I loved it, and women told me it really helped them navigate many life challenges other women who are not single moms could not understand. WTF Wednesdays has since retired, but I have used it as the inspiration for my next book! As a special thank-you for investing in *30-Day Kickass Single Mom Money Makeover*, I'm gifting you some of my favorite chapters in the forthcoming title, which is not yet available anywhere. Enjoy!

Dear Emma: WTF?!

My husband of 15 years just up and left me for a younger woman. Old story, I know—but I am still in shock. We have three kids ages 12, 10, and 9, a big mortgage in an excellent school district, and payments on two German cars—and I'm not talking Volkswagens. My husband owns a very successful small business, and I've been working part-time as an assistant at a local dentist's office. He is fighting me tooth and nail to pay as little child support and maintenance as he can. Needless to say, our lifestyle depends upon his income, yet I am having a hard time proving to the courts that he makes as much as he does because his is mostly a cash business.

I am so furious that he is able to walk away from his family and start life anew with little financial obligation to his kids—or me, for that matter. I am spending what little money I have on a divorce lawyer, but she tells me that even if the court orders him to pay more support, I will likely have to continue to fight to get it—and that may take years. I'm trying to find full-time work, but find myself spending hours on the internet and talking to friends and lawyers—all in an effort to figure out how to get more money out of this douchebag. It seems to make more financial sense to invest my time to try to get him to pay what he owes, rather than looking for a better job. Meanwhile, I am struggling to stay afloat so my kids can continue to live in the lifestyle my husband and I planned for them—much less plan for any future for my own later years.

What can I do?

Exhausted and Broke

Dear Broke,

Your signature says it all: you're exhausted! You and your kids need money. But more than that, you need energy to launch the fabulous new life you're about to create. There are two pieces of advice I can offer:

1. Fight on behalf of your kids.

2. Put your energy into only what you can control.

These may seem like conflicting messages, but they're not. On one hand, your ex certainly has a legal and moral obligation to support his children. Your responsibility as a parent is to care for your children to the best of your ability. As your lawyers said, this looks like it will be a long and ugly fight. Who knows how it will end.

Even assuming your ex will be forced to pay child support sooner or later, how will you pay the bills in the meantime?

And maybe just as importantly, how will you provide the emotional support that your kids need if you're spending all your energy being angry and fighting?

Enough lecturing. Here's what you will do:

Assess how you spend your energy. Notice this is Step No. 1. If you spend all your energy on revenge, getting your dues, and fighting your ex, that's all negative energy. What if you put that same energy into building your own career, wealth, and family? In that case, the sky is the limit! Meanwhile, fighting your ex may get you a court-ordered settlement and a moment of satisfaction. But he'll still be richer than you. And he'll still be screwing that hussy. You cannot control either fact.

As you move forward with your divorce, dig down deep into your soul and decide what you think is a fair sum. Rise above your anger. Take the necessary steps to get that number. Accept that you may not.

Now, make a plan to support your kids on your own financially. Does this mean a full-time assistant job? Pursue another career? Go back to school for advanced degrees? Build a work-at-home career?

Accept that you will likely be broke for a while. Mothers

usually are after divorce. But this will be temporary if you decide that it will be temporary.

Get a grip on your expenses. You cannot afford your sweet address anymore. That is sad, but even sadder would be to stay put in an abode that you will likely be kicked out of by your bank. That Benz? Swap it out for a Hyundai. Is there a way you can rent or buy and still stay in your school district? Get serious and practical. You may have to make some very hard decisions that will be painful in the short-term. Think about the long-term.

Accept that your lifestyle will change. You are no longer rich like you used to be (and I don't care if you classified yourself as "middle class." The lifestyle you described puts you in the upper .001 percent of the global population. Consider that for a second.). Accept that this is okay. It may be better than okay. It seems there was a lot of denial going on in your life. You were surprised that your husband was unhappy in your marriage. You were surprised to find out he is a dick. You were also surprised that your lifestyle was precarious. Living squarely within reality comes with it a liberty that money cannot buy. This is one of the most important lessons you can teach your children.

Accept that you are now free to build any lifestyle you want.

Remember my mantra: the best revenge is a life well lived.

XO,

Emma

Dear Emma, WTF?!

I'm a reasonably happily married mom, and one of my best friends is a single mom. We both have two kids. We go way back to high school and are more like sisters. I feel very close to her. But there is one thorn in my craw when it comes to that relationship, and that is money.

We don't talk about exactly how much we earn, but I estimate that between her child support and successful career as an industrial designer, her income is maybe only slightly less than what my husband and I earn together—maybe even the same. Yet she is constantly screaming poverty and makes snide remarks about how much wealthier (she thinks) my husband and I are.

For example, I drive an Audi. I really enjoy having a nice car and that is one of the few things my husband and I chose to splurge on. Same with international travel. But otherwise, we live very frugally, nearly always cook at home, stick to a budget, and rarely indulge in impulse buys.

Meanwhile, my friend drives a beat-up Dodge minivan that is constantly in need of repair, and yet her house is overflowing with the spoils of her frequent shopping trips. Barely used cosmetics spill out of her bathroom cabinets, her and her children's closets are bursting with clothes—many still bearing tags—and she throws out far more food than she eats.

And yet she has the nerve to make comments like, "Would you mind driving to dinner tonight? I know it's my turn, but the van is in the shop again—you know how it is for single moms!" and "Boy, I'd love to take my kids to Italy too, but there is no way I could afford that on one income. Your kids are so lucky that they can take a trip like that."

I feel like she is jealous of my lifestyle, which would be tricky if I actually had more money than she does—but I don't! Please stop me from killing her.

Frustrated in Phoenix

Dear Frustrated,

Sounds like your bestie has a case of single-mom syndrome. Symptoms include self-pity, refusal to take responsibility for one's actions, and being annoying—all in the name of her family status.

Here's what you do:

Take away her excuses. You go way back, and you say you are very close. I appreciate that every relationship has its boundaries, and in this case, you don't share financial information.

That's over.

Next time you two get together and share a bottle of Chardonnay and she starts in on her poverty story, treat her to a smackdown. Say: "Listen, I'm not so sure that I have more money than you do. Let's just lay things out here for the sake of our friendship. This is how much Tom and I brought in last year. How much do you make? How much child support do you get?"

This makes her face her reality in cold, hard numbers—and puts those numbers into a greater context. In this case, the context proves that she is a high earner. Can't argue with numbers!

Then say: "I appreciate that it must be overwhelming sometimes to parent solo. But I worry that you are using your single-mom status to limit yourself. You are so smart and successful, and have such great kids; it breaks my heart when you often say things like, 'Oh, I can't do XYZ for my kids because I'm a single mom.' You are so much better than that! I want more for you."

This shows her that you're coming to her from a place of love and friendship. It also sets some boundaries in the relationship. You're telling her that you are no fool, and you won't let her try to make you feel guilty about your choices. This talk can be a real gift to set her free from her own self-doubt—not to mention to shut up already and save the friendship!

XO,

Emma

Dear Emma, WTF?!

Four years after my divorce, I finally felt confident enough to get out of my yoga pants, buy some decent panties, and date. It was horrifying at first. For so long, I felt unattractive, unsexy (I mean, I'd never dated as a mom!), and totally clueless about navigating the singles scene in this crazy digital world.

But after a few weird OkCupid dates, I got into the swing of things and am having SO.MUCH.FUN. Why doesn't anyone tell you how awesome post-divorce sex is? The health department should run a PSA on the dangers of its addictiveness!

But here comes the pickle: in my spree of fun dates and casual hookups, I had a wonderful date with one very sexy, smart, and interesting single dad. In one very intense evening, we really connected—intellectually, emotionally, and sexually. Also, he makes total sense, is just a few years older than me, and is in a similar place in his life as a parent and professional (big high-five when compared with the smoking losers and delicious younger dudes I've been sampling).

So what's the problem?

After our one, admittedly magical, date, it has been a nonstop stream of texts, suggestions I meet his son, and long-term plans for our future. All I want to do is block him from my phone and keep whoring around!

But I worry: Shouldn't I give this guy a chance? I mean, he really is so great. What if I regret not pursuing him just because he's a little too much, too soon? Trust me: if my first date is any indication, this guy is a catch! But I went through utter hell to get to this place where I feel confident and sexy and feel like I can take on the world. I want to enjoy it. I should enjoy it, right? So why do I worry about regret?

Confused in Culver City

Dear Culver,

There is a mistress in every relationship. Her name is Time-Place. Time-Place can bring together two mismatched people for a bout of perfect harmony. And Time-Place can send two terribly compatible lovers into opposite, ships-in-the-night directions.

You and this man may be thwarted by Time-Place. You're having a blissful moment of post-divorce high. You have emerged from the horrors that is marital meltdown, and now have risen, a phoenix of sexual confidence. It's no wonder this man—and all these many, many other men—is drawn to you. You're on fire! And it doesn't hurt that you couldn't give a shit about any of them, creating an intoxicating recipe for their desire.

But an interesting thing is at play. Your powerful confidence both attracts this man and also makes him very insecure. He senses how hot you are and knows he must sink his clingy claws into your supple flesh before you skip off to enjoy the pleasures of the many other men in your wake. But instead of seducing you, he treats you like a needy, pathetic woman—one who wants nothing but the security of a monogamous relationship at any price.

That's not where you are.

But that's where he is.

Who could blame you for wanting to bolt? If there's nothing more seductive than a confident, ambivalent women, then there's no bigger boner killer than a needy man. You cannot commit to that! You would resent him from the start.

You worry that you should ignore your instincts to call it off, and lock down this good man. Honey, that smacks of a scarcity mentality that is so prevalent when it comes to single moms and romance. The world tells women: "There are no good men out there at this stage. When you find a decent one, lock him down! Do not let him get away! You will never find anyone better—ever!"

That mentality is compatible with the victim mentality of "there is only finite love in the world. You have but one—or few—soul connections. Rejecting any of them is ungrateful, and you will be punished."

In reality, there is infinite love. Infinite connection. Infinite passion, men, and love.

You are entitled to all the love, passion, fun, commitment, and variety that you desire. Do not get sucked into the miasma of single-mom dating messages.

As for your dude-in-pursuit, why not keep an open mind? First impressions—both good and bad—are nothing on which to make commitments. And so you will go on another date with this wonderful man. You will go on another date with this man for three reasons: 1) he is wonderful and you enjoy his company; 2) you need to know for sure that you do not want to date him; and 3) after an unusually special date, it is the honest thing to give it another shot out of respect for your feelings. This will make it easier to keep the door open for another moment for Time-Place to do her thing. And maybe that day—months or years from now—will be your moment together.

Or not.

XO,

Emma

Dear Emma, WTF?!

I really enjoy your blog, but I'm getting sick of your snotty advice. Sure, you've got it all going on: your great career and your beautiful kids and your fabulous life in New York. Well, guess what? Not everyone had all the advantages you did. We all can't just become successful entrepreneurs hiring house cleaners and laundry service and babysitters while we go partying with our slutty single-mom girlfriends on weeknights.

I'm 24 and I have three kids ages 5 and under by two different guys—neither of whom is around. I always dreamed of becoming a teacher and had really good grades in high school. But instead of going to college, I got pregnant. I live in a small town with a terrible economy and the only job I can find is at a daycare where I barely make enough money to get by. I would love to move to a bigger city—one with a university—get a teaching degree, and start a new life around interesting people doing interesting things. But my whole family is here, and this is all my kids know. I'm stuck, and I don't need you rubbing my face with your blog posts three times a week. In fact, most single moms would identify with me more than you. Go to hell.

Irate in Iowa

Dear Irate,

Every night when I tuck my kids into bed, we do what we call, "SayWhatWe'reGratefulFor" (all in one breath, as it's been known since my kids could talk). We take turns listing a few things that we appreciate in our lives. With my daughter, I often include this:

"I'm grateful that we live in a time and place where women can do whatever we want."

Our grateful exercise is about reminding ourselves of how rich we are. I also use it to rid myself of excuses. If I recognize how abundant my life is, I find few reasons not to be happy.

On reading your letter, my first impulse was to give you a rundown of all the hard knocks I've suffered in life, and then tell you how I pulled myself up by my bootstraps and assure you that, *Yes, you can do it too!* And all of that would be accurate, but here's the thing: you're right. I *do* have something that many people don't have: I had a mother and grandparents and aunts and uncles who supported my dreams to go on and do great things, even if we were all in a small town where things were far less than perfect and no one was doing anything that I thought was exciting. I had people who expected me to be who I wanted to be.

I can tell by your writing that you are very, very bright. You have a big personality (who you telling to go to hell?!), and you have big dreams. Plus, you're pissed. This all makes for the momentum you need to make a change. Whatever happens next will be scary. You relocate with your kids, you move away from everything you know, and you risk falling on your face. Scary! Stay put, and you risk hating yourself for the rest of your life for not living out your dream, becoming a (even more?) bitter person and mother and set forth the cycle of poverty and blame and excuses for your children. WAY SCARIER, right?

So here's what you will do:

1. Decide where you're moving. Not where you'd like to move. Where you *will* move. The only criteria

are that a) the town has a university with a teaching program, and b) you want to move there.

2. Make an appointment and go to that university within the next three weeks. Talk to the dean of admissions. Meet with someone in financial aid. Get a grip on what it will take to go there financially and logistically.

3. Walk around the campus. Walk around the neighborhoods. Imagine what it will be like to live there. Look at the people. Won't they be cool to know? Take your kids. Talk about what it will be like to go to school there, play in the parks, eat in the restaurants. See it and feel it. This will be your new life.

4. Make a plan. Not a 10-year-maybe-if-I'm-lucky plan. A real plan for within one year from now. Twelve months. Your plan will include making it happen financially—rent, a new job, and school for your kids and you. The plan will include you envisioning packing a moving truck, saying goodbye to your friends and old life, loading the kids up, and the four of you driving down the freeway toward your dreams. Your vision will feel scary and thrilling and

hopeful and even scarier. You will think of driving that moving truck down the freeway and feeling and thinking all of those things. The sun will be shining and you and your kids will be laughing.

5. Read stories. Stories about people overcoming adversity. Oprah, J. K. Rowling, Jay-Z, David Geffen. Google "true rags-to-riches stories" and spend the evening reading what you find. Before the end of the week, being poor in America with dreams of teaching in a city can become a normal, everyday thing.

6. Only tell your plan to a very few select people. Not people who may be jealous or doubtful and will steal your thunder. Maybe you don't have anyone like that. So you will email me, and I will forgive you for telling me to fuck off and I will write you back. You can join Millionaire Single Moms on Facebook, and we will listen to and encourage you.

7. Take a moment and be grateful. Grateful that you are smart and willful and a determined mother. Be grateful that you have a city and education and career that you can dream about. Be grateful that you live in a time and place where, as women, we can do whatever we want.

8.   You will do it. And it will be so, so hard. And you will cry and want to give up. And then it will be okay. And you will not be able to believe that you ever thought about staying in your hometown.

9.   When you are on your feet, you will fly to New York and we will go out drinking. On a weeknight.

XO,

Emma

Dear Emma, WTF?!

I divorced three years ago after 10 years with a man who barely worked and was constantly promising to make good on a variety of schemes and scams such as home security system pyramid schemes, flipping short-sale condos, buying a share of a beer distributorship, etc. When we met, I had an associate's degree and worked as a nurse's aid. Our finances were a constant source of stress, to say the least. I felt totally out of control and worried all the time about money.

Now, money is still tight, but I earned a nursing degree and am able to support myself and daughter by working as a registered nurse in a hospital. I am continuing to go to school with the goal of being a physician's assistant, where I can make a very comfortable living doing work that I am very good at and love. This is the first time in my life that I feel very strong and confident as a professional person, and I actually love paying the bills each month—because I always have enough money!

My big problem in life? I have a rich boyfriend. He is 10 years older, a successful entrepreneur, and semiretired. By all measures, he's a great guy. He totally adores me and my daughter, treats us incredibly well, and is proud to be part of my life—and me of his. We connect emotionally, intellectually, and sexually and enjoy a lot of the same things. Sometimes I can hardly believe that such a successful man loves me so much, especially after my marriage to a deadbeat. We are discussing a future together, and that is where the problems start.

He is looking forward to lots of travel, weekends at his lake house, and time with friends. It seems he assumes I will join him on all these adventures, which sound fantastic, except that they don't work with my professional plans. His attitude is, "Why work when you don't have to?" But I WANT to work. I love having my financial independence, serving my patients, working on a team with my colleagues, and building a career.

That is not to say that I don't enjoy all the material trappings that come with his money. I am human, after all. But I'm also starting to resent him and his wealth.

What should I do?

Frustrated in Fresno

Dear Frustrated,

Here are some truths:

1. There are lots of layers of a relationship: the two people's souls, the way they jibe when they spend time together, families, geography, timeline of their lives. Everything has to fit together, more or less, to make things work out long-term.

2. Money is power. You have felt powerless because of the lack of money in a relationship (your marriage), the joys of money power, by earning it yourself. Your boyfriend has more money than you. There is often the assumption that the person with less money morphs their life into that of the person with more money. You feel the pressure of that presumption.

3. There is more love in the universe than any of us can
    fathom.

In rebuilding your family's life post-divorce, you have discovered quite possibly the greatest power of all: your own inner resolve that allowed you to discover your greatest strengths and capitalize on them for the greater good. This power provides the joy you find in nursing, benefits the patients and businesses with whom you work, and benefits you and your daughter financially. That thrill you feel each month paying bills, going to work every week, waking each morning, and looking forward to your day—you have found a groove that few people in this world discover. Do not undervalue it.

There's another joy at play here: that of romantic love. There's a reason there are countless poems, operas, epic novels, and bump-and-grind jams devoted to love between a man and a woman, and not to nursing. This love is so powerful and feels so special that we sense it will never come again. And when it *is* with a person we deem to be glamorous or better than us, it seems such a precious commodity that we must sacrifice all to capture it—forever.

To which I say: let that shit go. The universe is abundant with love. Look around you! Everywhere you look, people are falling in love! They're flirting and swooning and hooking up. Sure, they're also crying and lonely and breaking each other's hearts. And then they pick themselves up and start again.

Your boyfriend is no doubt a good person. But he's also a powerful person with a powerful commodity—money. Question his dismissal of the need to work. After all, he succeeded in business because of his own passions and joy. Why would he want to rob you of that experience?

And to you I ask: Do you see that he's asking you to be dependent on him? You were once dependent on a poor man. Will being dependent on a rich man be better? Also, do you feel you deserve to be with someone who appreciates the very things you love about yourself? In addition to his appreciation of your daughter, your interests, and your sexuality, you deserve to be with a man who admires and respects your professional accomplishments and ambitions. That's part of the essence of your best self. On many levels, this guy offers a great package. But dig a little deeper and you will see there's a critical piece missing. And then you may tap into that deeper place and use that confidence and strength to know that other, different, and better love awaits you.

XO,

Emma

Dear Emma, WTF?!

When my daughter was 6 months old, her dad left and more or less never showed up again.

There were a few visits for a few years, and a couple of visits to family court for child support; but since then, we have not heard from or seen him. My daughter is now 8 years old.

We don't talk about it much and I feel like it isn't such a huge deal. She's a great kid—does well in school, has lots of friends, and is polite. We are close with my parents and siblings, who live nearby. I am glad that I get her all to myself and don't have to share custody like some of my divorced friends. Sometimes people say things to me like, "I feel so bad for her that she doesn't know her father." She never mentions her dad, and I feel like she doesn't care. She doesn't know any different. What should I tell all these rude people who judge our situation?

Defensive in Dallas

Dear Defensive,

I'm not worried about your rude neighbors. I'm worried about you and your daughter. When a parent is absent from a child's life—no matter by choice, imprisonment, or death—it is a loss. It is a loss for that child and a loss for those who love her.

We are all socially conditioned and predisposed with a deep need to know both our mother and our father. Socially, it's easy to understand that the majority of people grow up living with both a mother and a father—and nearly everyone else knows both parents. That's the norm. Your daughter is very aware that her family doesn't look like other families. She understands deeply that most of her friends have relationships with their dads and she doesn't.

We are each biologically half our mothers and fathers. Humans have an intrinsic need for family. We yearn to know our relatives so we can better know ourselves. When we are raised apart from our families, homelands, and extended cultures, there's a sense of loss that transcends our daily experience. This explains why people who are adopted are compelled to find their birth parents—no matter how wonderful their adoptive families are. This also explains why humans are driven to visit their ancestral homelands, even when they are removed from the place by generations.

Not every person will know both their parents. This is a fact. This does not mean that your daughter does not have a fantastic life, or that she is not a wonderful child who will grow up to be a happy, productive, and lovely adult.

But those things do not preclude loss and grief. Your daughter has experienced a great loss. She does not know her father. She is different from other kids. And she also has a mother who dismisses this loss. When grief is ignored or belittled, it creates shame. I don't care what your daughter expresses outwardly—she is deeply affected by this situation.

Before you can help your child, you must address your own loss and grief. When your ex-husband left and abandoned your daughter, he also abandoned you—both as a husband, but more to the point here, as a co-parent. You also suffered a loss in that you do not have someone to help raise your daughter—even if it means separately as divorced parents. You do not have anyone to enjoy their sweet habits or to commiserate on the daily challenges of parenthood. You do not get to enjoy a co-parenting arrangement that gives you a break. Most of all, you suffer because deep down you know your daughter is hurt. That, for any mother, is devastating.

This situation can be changed. But you must take action.

First, you must recognize the situation for what it is: a huge, giant, grave loss. It is not your fault. It is life. But it is your responsibility as a parent to address it. First, acknowledge how this has affected you personally. Lean into that pain. Right now, you are avoiding that pain, which is why you're dismissing it in your daughter. Just sit with it. Cry, scream, punch your mattress, or write him an angry letter you never send. Whatever is your way, go there.

Then, recognize that he is human. When a parent abandons a child, that parent is deeply wounded. There's a reason they cannot fulfill their responsibility. They don't recognize they are worthy of being needed or can bring value to another person's life. Your ex misses out—in a very major way—on the joy of raising and loving his child. He also suffers knowing that he deeply hurts her. Every day.

Recognizing this is part of the process of forgiveness. It involves empathy and grace. It will take time. But you must get there—for your sake, and that of your daughter's.

While you work through that, you must now face your daughter.

Talk with her. Say: "I've been thinking a lot about your dad.

I imagine you do too. How do you feel about the fact that you don't know him?"

Ask her how she feels when she visits friends who live with their dads—or have visitation schedules with both their divorced parents. Tell her about her father, how you met him, what you liked and loved about him. Tell her stories about your time with him, and stories he told you about his life. Tell her about his family and the jokes he told. Ask her what she'd like to know about him. Answer honestly— including the part where he left. And why he doesn't call. If you don't know how to answer some questions, say so. "I wish I knew, but I don't."

That is just the first conversation.

Have another the next week.

And the next.

You may not have weekly conversations about your daughter's father for the rest of your lives, but get into a habit of talking about him. About her father. Give her permission to ask, to feel. Do not sugarcoat the information or your own feelings. Especially as she gets older, tell her what really went down and how absolutely infuriated you were—and maybe still are. By recognizing your feelings and sharing them honestly with her, you give her permission to recognize and honor her own complex and human feelings.

Only then can both of you move forward with the full, wonderful, and complex life you were meant to have.

XO,

Emma

Dear Emma, WTF?!

I am going through a nasty divorce—custody battles, bitter fighting over money. You name it. My kids are 5 and 11.

Until the last six months, I was really together: successful in my career as an administrator at a nonprofit, totally organized at home, and on top of my kids' activities/homework/ appointments.

Recently, I can hardly recognize myself. Last week, I found a school lunch that somehow made its way under my daughter's bed and festered into a stinky, indeterminable compost. I've left my 5-year-old home alone, unattended for at least half an hour, and I completely spaced about one of his soccer matches. Then, the other day, I was trying to squeeze in a business call when my son wandered into the room and a louse crawled out of his hair! I actually screamed right into the phone with my boss. I was horrified.

Then, there is the fact that I have gained 17 pounds in the past half year, the house is more or less always in disarray, and despite my self-promises to the contrary, I continue to indulge in arguments with my kids' father—right in front of them.

I worry that divorce has turned me into a really lousy mom, crazy person, and incompetent professional. I am so ashamed of myself. Can I turn this around?

Battling It Out in British Columbia

Dear B.C.,

First, I bet every person who has gone through divorce can identify with this letter. You know who else can identify with this letter?

Pretty much everyone.

Let me tell you a story. One afternoon when my daughter

was about 5 or 6 months old, she dozed off on my bed. She was a roly-poly little thing—literally rolling around the entirety of the living room instead of crawling. I knew this. I also knew that those naps provided elusive me-time. And so, I negligently let her snooze on the bed while I jumped in the shower.

A few minutes later, I heard muffled screams, which I found—upon bursting out of the shower—were from my tiny baby, face down on the hardwood floors. In the two seconds between the time she fell and when I scooped her up, an egg-size purple bump had popped up between her eyes.

I was sick.

Was I a stressed-out, sleep-deprived new mom? Maybe. Was I a lazy, negligent mom for selfishly not moving her sleeping baby and sneaking off to the steamy luxury of a solitary shower? Perhaps. I recall those days as my giddiest. And also some of my most human.

Fast-forward a couple years, and I was in the throes of divorce. This time was a blur. But I remember this:

My son, age one, went to the counter and pulled down the

French press full of scalding coffee. He had an armful of blisters to show for it.

I spanked my kids.

More than once, I 100 percent completely spaced on meetings/deadlines/appointments—so unusual for me, I thought for sure I had suffered a neurological disorder.

Sent my kids to daycare in less-than-clean clothes.

Wore the same (less-than-clean) clothes four days in a row.

Served (really, really delicious) food that may or may not have been in the fridge too long.

That was three or four years ago. Two days ago? Had a big fight with the ex in the lobby of my building—just as the cool (and sweet) jewelry-designer neighbor and her baby were walking in. Stay classy, Emma!

My point is twofold:

1. You are human. Humans are not perfect. Erase from your mind the idea that there's such a thing as a perfect mom. We are all so, so deeply flawed. Effed up, really! Life gets so much easier if you wake up in the morning and accept as truth that you will in some

way damage your children. I give you permission to damage them. Try your best, and know that you will still fail. Lice? Part of childhood. Stop taking it all so personally! You're not that special!

2. Divorce is a mother. It dissolves all sense of control over your life. If you don't unravel during your split, you *will* unravel—10 times, as that shit ferments— later. If you weren't somehow being a lesser mom, then something would be amiss. And what you describe is safely within the bounds of losing your mind temporarily while you get through this mess.

So what to do:

1. Take a cold, hard look at your divorce proceedings. These things can go on and on until your kids leave the house and beyond. Take a real, hard, cost-benefit analysis of the time, energy, money, and headspace you spend thinking about your divorce, talking about it with anyone who listens, arguing with your ex in your mind—not to mention the actual time you spend communicating with your lawyer and in court! Is it time to let some of it go and just wrap it up already?

2. Give yourself a break. I'm not one for encouraging all this retail therapy (which has its place, don't get me wrong) or slurping back bottles of wine or booking spa weekends when things get tough. Instead, set your jaw and when something goes amuck, roll with it and forgive yourself.

3. Stay away from social media, as well as all other media. More families' homes look like yours and mine, but we feel bad about it because our homes don't look like Instagram or Facebook families. Which are different from real families. Guilt and shame ensue.

4. You need a good friend. Someone you can laugh and share with, who makes you feel normal. Because all of this is normal. Shame is the enemy.

5. Get help. I'm thinking a housekeeper and more childcare. Outsource all these little things that you're beating yourself up over. Then you can focus on the important stuff—like enjoying your kids, getting through and over the end of your marriage, and picking nits.

6. Take care of yourself. Self-care is no joke. This week, start an exercise routine. This is not just to address

the extra weight, but to carve out time for yourself to do something positive and healthy. Identify three healthy things you will do each week to be kind to yourself: spend time with friends (at your homes, out, on the phone, or FaceTime), enjoy nature, reserve 20 minutes of quiet time alone each evening or morning, or eat your favorite fruit while watching a great Netflix show.

7. Be grateful. You'll notice that I include this advice in my work often, and there is a reason: science proves it makes us happier and healthier and gives us better relationships. Writing down even a few things you're thankful for each day shifts your perspective on your life and world.

8. Hang tight. This, too, shall pass. Really. You will look back at this time in months and years and not even recognize yourself.

XO,

Emma

In Gratitude

This book could not have been possible without the love of the following beautiful people who support me, and our greater mission of gender equality for single mothers—and women everywhere. Thank you all for kicking so much ass.

Mitch Fields, Christelyn Karazan, Camille Johnson, Helena and Lucas, Molly Ward, Tanya Van Court, Cameron Huddleston Lebedinsky, Lauren Sweeney, Louise Sloan, Amanda Kingsbury, Michelle Jackson, Tiffany Hugo Horsley, Elsa Carlson, Hollie Graham, Loren Guillory, Leah Starin, Jess Coleman, Melinda Martin, Shayla Raquel, Bethany Major, Frank Eakin, Erin Lowrey, Bethany Major, Amy Johnson, Kirsten Searer, Amanda Kracen, Jenny Hadad, Penny Makras, Trae Bodge, Katie Wilson, Ashley Bernardi, Nicole Earl, John R. Schneider, Lauren Greutman, Tracy Thorner Morris, Nicole Earl,

Stephanie Hughes, Zabrina Rodriguez, Jayme Moebius, Brittany Searle, Alicia LaPeruta, Brooke Cormack, Sarah Mitchell, Candace Spencer, Angela Monique Martinez, Jessica Chandrasekharan, Janice L., Nikki White, Lynsey Ross Lund, Nicole Callender, Hanna Riggins, Kimberly Dashley, Megan Elizabeth Booth, Allison Gates, Amanda Melendez, Jen McLean, Amy Pignatella Cain, Megan J Borsh, Rhiannon L. Tunnell, Katrina Peterson, Laura Kathleen, Brittany Cheek, Diane Barrett, Karen Vos, Stacey L. Emerson, Leda Anagnostopoulos, Victoria Hermosillo, Lindsay A. Harrington, Pauline Sila, Alana Nicole, Denise Gonyea, Betsy S. Gilman-Robbins, Elizabeth Kilmer, Cara Grib, Hannah May Ostrander, Melissa Ann-Oppelt Taylor, Pattina Pecarovich, Tania Henriquez, Fallon Havens, Valerie Shull, Mamod Saj, Julie M. Wolfe Keiko Katayama, Michelle Davis, Ph.D., and all the members of Millionaire Single Moms on Facebook—I could not have done it without our incredible community!

---- ☆ ----

ABOUT THE AUTHOR
Emma Johnson

 Hey! I'm Emma Johnson, founder of Wealthysinglemommy.com, the largest platform for single moms in the world. My first book, *The Kickass Single Mom,* was a #1 bestseller and featured in the New York Times, Wall Street Journal, The Doctors, Oprah.com, MONEY, TIME, and other fabulous places. Before I was a blogger, I was a full-time business journalist. Nothing makes me angrier than women being broke. It is my highest priority goal on this planet to help women earn, save, and invest more money. Without money, you have no power. Without our own money, women as a gender will never have equal power. I want you to have power! Your power is my power and is every woman's power. Let's do this!

CONNECT WITH THE AUTHOR
Emma Johnson

Wealthysinglemommy.com

Millionaire Single Moms
group on Facebook

Instagram.com/thejohnsonemma

Linkedin.com/in/emmajohnson

YouTube.com/Wealthysinglemommy

Like a Mother, my award-winning podcast on iTunes

Leave a Review

If you enjoyed this book, please write a review on Amazon
and Goodreads! Reviews help authors reach new readers.

Amazon: amazon.com/gp/product/B07JH2MZ7W

Goodreads: goodreads.com/book/show/42380881-30-day-
kickass-single-mom-money-makeover